"Don't You Hate It When..."

HOW TO SOLVE A GARDENER'S LITTLE IRRITATIONS

BY MIKE HIBBARD

ILLUSTRATED BY GAIL K. FURGAL

INTRODUCTION BY MAR

PINKHAM PUBLISI

"Don't You Hate It When..."

HOW TO SOLVE A GARDENER'S LITTLE IRRITATIONS

BY MIKE HIBBARD

Pinkham
PUBLISHING

For more of our products visit www.maryellenproducts.com
PO BOX 390221, EDINA, MN 55439-0221 • 800-328-6294

PRINTED IN THE UNITED STATES OF AMERICA First Printing: March, 2006
ISBN 13: 978-0-941298-41-4; ISBN 10: 0-941298-41-8

This book is dedicated to:

Fred Glasoe, a great science teacher, horticulturist and gardener. He was the principal at the military school I attended in Iwankuni, Japan, and I met him when I was sent to the principal's office—though I can't remember why! When our paths crossed again years later, he taught me the art of horticulture;

The Bachman family, who have encouraged me to do what I love since I was 15;

My grandmother who didn't mind my digging in her garden.

And to all of the gardeners who taught me their acquired wisdom from hands-on experience long before all the newfangled chemical formulas and garden gadgets came to market. I thank them and I have tried to pass along their common sense and practical advice through my radio show and now I am delighted to do so with this book. I hope it solves many gardeners' little irritations.

Mike

Introduction

I took up gardening in 1990. From the minute I planted my first rose bush, there was hardly a moment when gardening wasn't on my mind. My plans got more and more elaborate. It got to the point where I was gardening in my dreams.

(Don't you hate it when you think the weeding is done and then you wake up?)

In 1996 I invited Mike Hibbard—a radio and television personality and the horticulturist from Bachman's, a large garden center in Minneapolis—to be a regular on my HGTV show, *TIPical Mary Ellen*. I thought maybe he could tell me how I could grow palm trees in my back yard in Minnesota.

(Don't you hate it when plants you like won't grow in your zone?)

Well, Mike is a practical guy. He told me to forget about the palm trees. But he's also imaginative. He showed me how I could be successful growing tropical flowers in zone 4. Thanks to what I've learned from him, I've stopped wasting time and money making mistakes in my garden. Of course, I'm still spending, but not on mistakes.

(Don't you hate it when something that's fun becomes an addiction?)

I wouldn't know where to start telling you all that I've learned from Mike. And I certainly couldn't tell you as well as he could. So I thought it was best for him to tell you himself. Enjoy this book. You'll get a lot out of it, and so will your garden.

Mary Ellen

Please note: Growing conditions vary, and individual plants react differently to different formulas. So test any recipe in this book on a small portion of any plant before you apply the full dosage.

(Don't you hate it when you have to cover your backside with disclaimers?)

Contents

Flowers   **1**

Crops   **27**

Lawns, Shrubs, and Trees   **47**

Root Cuttings, Seeds, and Seedlings   **67**

Containers, Cut Flowers, and Houseplants   **75**

Equipment   **95**

Chores   **117**

Disease, Insects, and Weather   **145**

Wildlife and Birds   **169**

Index   **182**

**Chapter 1
Flowers**

ANNUALS AND PERENNIALS

Don't You Hate It When...

Plants bloom too early and die

• Don't rush the season and start planting heat-loving plants because of a few warm days. Unpredictable spring weather cycles (hot one day, cold the next) can kill your plants. While pansies, violas, snapdragons, and sweet peas are among the plants that can be planted early, impatiens, begonias, and coleus need warmer weather.

• Check your garden center to see how to treat the plants you like. If they're in a greenhouse, chances are that they don't like cool nights. But the plants that have been put outside at the garden center should be able to withstand lower temperatures.

It takes so long to plant annuals

• Plant annuals that are in cell packs easily with a bulb planter. First prepare the holes by pushing the bulb planter into the ground, twisting it a few times, then placing the little plants into the soil.

Potted perennials are on sale in the fall but you don't have time to plant them

• Buy the bargains, and put the pots in an empty garden spot for a winter vacation. Cover them with compost in the fall and then with marsh hay after the ground freezes. In the spring you'll look forward to planting your good buys.

You don't know how to separate daylily roots for planting

• In early August, the best time for this task, water the plant well the night before. Dig up the plant with a garden fork, wash the dirt away from the roots with a hose, and with the palm of your hand, gently roll the clean roots back and forth on the ground until they separate. Each fan of leaves will grow into a new clump. Trim each fan so 6–8" of leaf remains. Plant immediately in a sunny spot and water well.

Your lavender doesn't thrive

• Lavender doesn't like fertilizer, and after spring rains, it likes well-drained (dry) soil. So the key to success is poor soil. Plant it where it will get a full day of hot sun together with plants that like similar conditions (straw flowers, moss roses, and cleome), and when the weather turns dry in mid-summer, don't water it as you would other plants.

• Don't count on keeping the plant through the winter in a northern garden.

• Alternatively, use a lavender look-alike such as Salvia "May Night" *S. x superba* "Mainacht."

Peony blooms don't last

• Cut the flowers in the garden when the blooms are soft and the size of a ping-pong ball. (The trick is to pick buds that are about to open). Put them in a vase of water. In two or three days, they'll open up.

• When the buds are 1–1½" big, you can wrap the stemmed flowers in wet newspaper, place them in a plastic bag, refrigerate the bag, and remove only a few stems at a time to display in a vase. The refrigerated bundle will last over a month, perhaps into July, if the fruit in the refrigerator is sealed tightly in plastic bags. (Fruit gives off a gas that will shorten the life of the flowers.)

• Peonies don't need ants to help open their buds. Ants are present to collect the sweet sap that is on the flower buds.

Peonies flop over

• Peony hoops are available in garden centers. But you can make your own with a 2' square piece of chicken wire and four stakes about 24" long. Put the stakes about 6" into the ground in a square pattern and attach the chicken wire to the top of the stakes, 18" from the ground. Make sure the peony stems grow through the wire.

• Or when the buds start to bloom, wrap twine around each plant about 6" from the top. Tie the twine tight enough so the stems will stand straight. The twine doesn't show through the leaves that will cover it.

• Or plant single peonies. They require no staking.

Tall phlox seedlings aren't as colorful as their parent plants

• When phlox go to seed, the vigorous seedlings—which are a washed-out pink—will eventually

5

choke out the more desirable plant. To avoid this, remove the blossoms when three-quarters of the flowers have finished blooming. Give these plants full sun, plenty of air, and moisture (without keeping them wet). Look for new mildew-resistant varieties, like "Volcano."

Perennials die back and leave dead space in the garden

• Use pots of annuals to fill in dead spaces or to cover flowers like Oriental poppies that become unattractive when they're dormant. Set the pots next to the fading flowers, but remove them by fall. Some plants, like poppies, grow a bit before winter and need some room.

• Or put plants in decorative pots and put them on bricks stacked to various heights. The pots are attractive, the plants won't get lost among the other plants, and the added dimension makes a garden look more interesting.

Nothing grows in hot spots

• Mandevilla vines are tropical treasures that are spectacular in any garden, with giant flowers that resemble giant morning glories. The pinks are especially pretty. They can be grown in containers on decks and patios, especially in hot sunny spots against the house where most plants don't thrive, and require a trellis or chicken wire for their vines to twine around. They can be allowed to get dry between waterings because they have a tuberous root system, but the constant show of bloom requires a lot of energy, so they are heavy feeders. Give them a low-nitrogen liquid fertilizer alternating with a balanced 10-10-10 granular fertilizer. Though mostly pest-free, they can be attacked by aphids during summer months. In fall, cut back the vine, bring it inside, place it in a sunny window and cut back on watering. Let the plant go semi-dormant until mid-March, than give it more water and a little food. Bring it outside when the weather turns warm.

Fieldstone walls look cold and gray

• Liven up the wall with trailing nasturtiums, alyssum, and lobelia. Plant seeds into dampened sphagnum sheet moss, tuck the pieces of moss into the cracks and crevices of the wall, and water the plants regularly.

BULBS

You're confused about how to plant bulbs

• Most gardeners don't plant bulbs deep enough. Tulips should be planted 10" deep in the north, 6–7" in the south. Put daffodils 10–12" deep in the north, 8–10" deep in the south.

Bulb gardens don't look natural

• To make flowering bulbs look as if nature had put them there, they shouldn't be planted in neat rows but rather in circles or drifts in groups of six or more. To make a natural-looking drift, toss a bucket of golf balls into the air and plant two or three bulbs wherever a ball has landed. If two have landed together, plant four to six at the spot.

You can't get a great show on a budget

• Plant a hundred daffodils *Narcissus poeticus* "Pheasant's Eye" bulbs a year. Before long, you'll have an outstanding spring landscape. They grow naturally in seasonally moist pastures and near swampy land. A grassy meadow or a naturalized stream bank where other grasses and wildflowers will not compete for attention would be ideal. Buy bulbs in fall; plant them in a sunny spot in September.

There are dead spaces in your daffodil field

• To fill a grassy field, you should plant two or three hundred bulbs each year, but eventually, you won't remember where the existing daffodils are located and won't know where new ones should be placed. To have a stock of daffodils available to fill in the gaps, plant daffodil bulbs in nursery pots, then plant the pots in your vegetable garden. In the spring when you see bare spots, transplant the potted daffodils.

You're short of time to plant the fall bulbs

• Get the bed ready for fall bulbs at the same time as you are planting a new garden in the spring. Dig up the ground with a shovel to loosen the soil around the perennials, and then dig holes for the fall bulbs, putting the soil you remove into large-sized pots. Drop the full pots into the holes and plant with annuals. Come fall, lift the pots, plant the bulbs and then dump the soil from the pot over the holes.

You dig up bulbs because you forgot where they were

• Plant grape hyacinth bulbs over larger bulbs. They send up foliage in the fall, stay green all winter long, and blooms in the early spring. By the time the tulips and daffodils come out, the grape hyacinths are starting to go dormant, but they will be back in the fall to mark the beds.

You can't remember where new bulbs should be planted

• Plant gladiolus bulbs in the spring in the spots where tulips are dying back or in other vacant places. In the fall, dig up the gladiolus bulbs and replace them with new tulip bulbs.

• Use golf tees as plant markers.

• Or use clothespins.

• And hope you can remember where to find these tips.

You want to plant, but you don't have a bulb planter

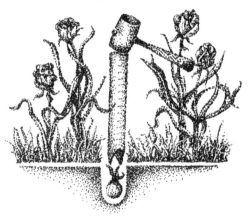

• Use a foot-long, 2½" in diameter, piece of PVC pipe instead. First, mark the pipe for inches, then make a cut on each side of the pipe that will stick into the soil. (This will make removing the compacted soil easier if it gets stuck). With a mallet, pound the pipe into the ground to the planting depth of the bulb, then pull it out. The soil will stay in the pipe, leaving a neat hole. Drop in the bulb, then hold the pipe over the hole and tap the side with the mallet so the soil falls back into the hole. If the soil won't come out, ram a copper pipe with a cap down the PVC pipe to knock it out.

You can't figure out which end of the bulb goes up

• Tear-shaped tulip and daffodil bulbs should be planted pointy end up. But when you're not sure which is the pointy end, plant the bulb on its side. (Even if planted upside down, a bulb will sprout and bloom, though later than usual.)

Spring bloom doesn't last long enough

• For maximum show, plant early, mid-season, and late varieties of tulips together so the bulb garden will have color over a long period in the spring. Do the same with daffodils.

• Or plant different bulbs in two layers to keep the flowering going. Place the larger ones about 10–12" deep and the smaller about 2–3" deep. Some large/small combinations that work well together: tulips/scilla, daffodils/crocus, hyacinth/ grape hyacinth, and allium/dwarf daffodils.

• Or use the three-layer plan. Make a hole 1' deep and 2' square.

First layer: Plant three large allium and up to 15 daffodils. Cover with 3" of soil, and work fertilizer in for the bulbs following instructions on the box.

Second layer: Plant about 20 tulips. If the two layers touch, that's okay; the bulbs will grow around each other. Cover with soil and fertilizer as before.

Third layer: Plant small bulbs such as crocus, grape hyacinth, species tulips, snowdrops, and mini daffodils—about 10 per square foot (about 40 in all). Repeat soil/fertilizer step. Water thoroughly and keep area moist until the ground freezes, then cover with leaves.

There's no room in the beds for early spring flowers

• There's always room for what many gardeners refer to as "special little" hardy bulbs. You'll find a wide selection in your garden center in the fall. They're little things that can make a big difference. Some suggestions:

• Plant blue *Scilla siberica* directly into the lawn about 3" deep. (See "Tiny spring bulbs take lots of time to plant," below) The little flowers en masse turn the lawn bright blue in early spring and complete their life cycle before you'll need to mow the lawn.

• Guinea-hen flower *Fritillaria meleagris* is underutilized. It brightens deciduous woodland before the leaves come out, looks terrific under birch trees, and won't be eaten by deer, which hate its skunky scent.

• Snowdrops *Galanthus* are an all-time favorite. They bloom when the snow is still on the ground.

Tiny spring bulbs take lots of time to plant

• To plant hundreds of small bulbs quickly, use a garden fork with tines. Stick it into the ground about 4" deep, rock it back and forth, then remove it. You'll have four holes that are just the right size into which to drop a bulb. Pinch the holes shut.

• Two ways to go even faster: Soften the ground by watering it the preceding day, and work with a partner. One person makes the holes and the other drops in the bulbs and pinches the holes shut. If you are working with a teenager who doesn't like to garden, the job may NOT go faster.

Daffodils and tulips die back and spoil the look of the garden

• Plant bulbs in the back of the garden bed or around spring perennials so the die-back will not be as noticeable. But don't remove any green leaves until the entire plant has turned brown, since they give the bulb its energy. When the brown leaves have been removed, plant annuals over bare spaces.

• Plant daffodil bulbs between daylilies. Daffodils will bloom in spring, and growing daylily foliage will hide their leaves as they die back.

• As few as 10 daffodils or tulips planted together can produce a spot of color, and they will be less unsightly when they're dying back if you plant them close to perennials that like dry soil. The perennials will hide the brown dying foliage.

You aren't sure when to pull the dying bulb foliage

• As soon as it pulls off without any resistance, go ahead and remove it.

Dahlias flop over

• Three-tiered metal tomato cages can be used to support dahlias and peonies.

Winter kills begonias and dahlias

• Plant them in large nursery pots in the spring, then put the pot directly into the garden when there is no longer any danger of frost.

(Be sure to check them daily for water needs and feed them regularly.) In the fall, you can just dig up the pot and store it for the winter indoors in a cool spot where the temperature is 40–45° F. Don't cut off foliage until it dries back and don't water plants once you've taken them indoors. In the spring, six weeks before you plan to put tuberous begonias outdoors (four weeks before for dahlias), water the pot. Set the begonias in an east window, the dahlias in a west or south one. When the plant has true leaves, give it water soluble fertilizer (but make the solution half strength).

You don't know how to keep bulbs for the winter

• Put small bulbs in egg cartons and larger ones in cardboard boxes (but never in plastic, which doesn't breathe). Cover the bulbs with peat moss. Write the name of the bulb on the carton with a permanent marker.

• Or treat the bulbs as annuals and replant new ones each fall.

• For great bargains on bulbs, wait until late fall to purchase tulips. Buy your bulbs from a local garden center rather than by mail. The bulbs most likely will be bigger.

You don't get bulbs planted before the ground freezes

• Lay an old electric blanket over the frozen ground. Cover it with several more blankets and turn the electric blanket on. When the soil has thawed the bulbs will be easy to plant.

• You can put tulips in the ground until the ground freezes, but if you don't get them planted in time, keep them in paper bags in the refrigerator crisper drawer. As soon as you can get into the ground in the early spring, preferably while there's still snow on the ground, dig a hole. Toss away any soft or spoiled bulbs and plant the rest. First cover them with soil, then pile as much snow as you can find on top of the soil, and put straw on top of that. The idea is to keep the ground cold, which helps grow roots on hardy bulbs. When the snow melts, the bulbs should bloom.

You're replanting an iris rhizome but you can't tell what color it is

• When a tall bearded iris is in bloom, tie yarn to a leaf. Color-code the yarns to indicate color or size. When you divide the rhizomes in August, you can sort and replant them according to your own design.

Cannas are late to bloom

• Cannas are tropical plants and grow where a lot of rainfall is followed by a dry spell in which they become semi-dormant. If they are stored when completely dormant, they will need extra time to start to grow and bloom. So, if you live where there are killing frosts and a short growing season, start them indoors a month before you set them outdoors and they'll start to bloom a month earlier.

Mike's Pick:
Easiest Canna to Maintain

• Choose cannas marked "self-cleaning." These will deadhead themselves, a great time- and energy-saver.

You can't tell which bulbs are which when stored

• Take digital pictures of each canna and dahlia in full bloom, then after the season, pack each bulb in a shoebox filled with vermiculite or dried peat moss. Affix the photo to the outside of the box so you know which box holds which.

• The easiest way to keep track of dahlias and other tubers is to write the name, size, or color of the flower right on the tuber. Use a permanent black marking pen with a fine point.

Gladiolus needs staking

• If you plant them 8–10" deep, staking won't be necessary.

Mike's Pick:
Favorite Lily for Shade

• **Try Martagon lilies, which are very happy in part shade. They grow best under the canopy of large trees, at the edge of a wooded area, or on the shady side of buildings.**

Lilies flop over

• They'll have less chance of flopping over if you put at least 6" of soil over the top of them.

• But, stake tall lilies so the wind doesn't snap off their tops. Use strips of an old T-shirt or pantyhose to tie the flower to the stake.

• Lilies are easy to grow if you remember this: They like their heads in the sun and their feet in the shade. Plant them among other plants so the base of the stem is protected from the sun.

ROSES

You don't have any luck propagating roses

• Try my grandmother's technique. None of her roses was grafted; they just grew on their own root. In June, cut the top 6" of a young green stem (not a brown woody one) just below a leaf. Remove all of the lower leaves on the stem, leaving only two to three leaves on the top. Soak the cutting in willow water overnight. (See page 68, "Root cuttings.") In the morning, stick the cutting in wet soil so the remaining leaves are just above the ground.

Grandma covered her cuttings with glass canning jars and left them alone until new growth started later in the summer. The soil should be loamy and amended with vermiculite; the cuttings should be in a protected area that is shaded in the afternoon. I like this method because once the cutting is planted into the garden you can pretty much ignore it. When the inside of the jar looks dry (there's no humidity inside of it), it's time to remove the jar and water. As soon as you're done watering, replace the jar.

• Or follow the above instructions, but instead of willow water use a rooting hormone and plant in a pot of seed starter mix instead of planting directly in the garden. Use plastic bags instead of a glass jar to cover the cutting to achieve a greenhouse effect.

You don't know how to keep shrub roses blooming

• Unlike older varieties that bloomed mainly in June, new ones often bloom from June to frost. However, they need regular deadheading to remove spent flowers so they'll continue producing a display of flowers.

Roses aren't thriving

• Give a rose bush a banana. Cut the peel in small pieces, then place it at the base of the bush and cover it with compost. Then eat the banana yourself. The potassium is good for you.

Thorns cut you when you're cleaning in between rose canes

• With duct tape, attach a table fork to the end of a short piece of broom or mop handle. It's a great tool for this job.

• Or vacuum up the debris with a shop vac.

Climbing roses aren't producing lots of blooms

• You'll see an abundance of flowers if you train climbing roses. They send out straight 10–12' canes, sometimes even longer. When you see a large cluster of buds on the tip—an indication that the cane has reached the end of its growth—bend the cane carefully so it is pointing down, and tie it to the trellis. Short side branches, each producing a cluster of buds, will start to grow from each leaf axil, the point where the leaf joins the stem. To support those blooms, feed the plant while it's flowering, up until mid-summer.

Mike's Pick:
Hardiest Shrub Roses

• "Winnipeg Parks" is only 24" high, has 2½" semi-double cherry red flowers, blooms from late spring to fall, and is hardy to zone 2. For a climbing shrub rose, try "Climbing Ramblin' Red Rose," an improved "Henry Kelsey." It grows 10' high, its double red flowers bloom from late spring to fall, and it is hardy to zone 3.

You don't know how to plant a new rose bush

• When planting a new rose, mix alfalfa mulch into the existing soil to supply organic matter and nutrients. Later in the summer, use alfalfa mulch to top-dress the rose bed. Work alfalfa mulch into the soil around established roses in the spring to re-introduce organic material. In spring and early summer, water them with alfalfa tea. To make the tea, fill a large glass loosely with alfalfa mulch and add enough warm water to fill the jar. Place the sealed jar in a sunny spot for three to five days. Strain the liquid through cheesecloth.

GROUND COVER

Digging out ground cover makes a bare spot

• If you want to divide existing ground cover to plant in other areas, first use a large step-on bulb planter to dig holes in the new area, then use the planter to pull out plugs. Dig into the middle of a cluster of ground cover rather than the sides, so the area won't look as disturbed, and refill the holes with compost. It'll fill in quickly.

Debris gets stuck in between ground cover

• Use a shop vac to tidy the area.

Mike's Pick:
Best Ground Cover

• Japanese spurge "Pachysandra" prefers shady areas, even under evergreens. (In the sun, it will yellow and burn, though it can survive in partial sun if the soil is rich and organic.) Planted about 12" apart, it will grow to 8" tall. It will spread its shiny green leaves at a moderate rate, sending out rhizomes that send up new plants. Take care with watering and feeding for the first two seasons and within two to three seasons you will have a lush, evergreen ground cover that requires little maintenance. But scale attack can turn pachysandra pale yellow; control this by spraying with a horticultural oil in the spring. The small white flowers may be hard to spot, but they send off a strong, sweet fragrance and en masse can smell as sweet as a rose garden. Great varieties include "Green Carpet," "Green Sheen," and "Variegata."

VINES

Morning glories take so long to flower

• Jump-start morning glories by planting them indoors two to three weeks before the last spring frost. Put the seeds in a kitchen strainer, pour 1 quart of boiling water over them, and then place the seeds in lukewarm water for several hours. Plant them in peat pots, two or three seeds in each. Keep the soil moist and place plants in a warm sunny spot. As seedlings grow, stake them if necessary. On warm spring days set the plants outside for a few hours to accustom them to the outdoors. When the soil is warm, plant the peat pots in the garden, preferably in a sunny spot where they can find some kind of support. Keep them moist and use a high nitrogen fertilizer for the first month, then a low nitrogen fertilizer. Poor soils will produce thin, scrappy plants but they will have many more flowers than pampered ones.

Vines don't grow quickly enough to provide "instant" screening and privacy

• Perennial vines take several years to establish a sufficient root system to produce desired top growth. While waiting for this to happen, provide immediate coverage by planting annuals such as morning glories, cup and saucer vines, black-eyed Susan vines and Mandevilla vines. You may have to repeat this for two or three years. It will take that long until the perennial can stand alone.

Vines in a window box have no support

• Use hemp twine to support vines like black-eyed Susan. Thumbtack one end of several strands to the side of the window box and the other ends to the side of the window frame near the top. The vine will grip the twine but it won't hold onto fishing line and dental floss, which some people try to use.

Sweet potato vines rot during the winter

• Store clean, dry tubers in brown paper bags with some dry peat moss and place them in the coolest part of the basement. Be very careful not to damage the tiny tuber eyes or they will not sprout. Pot them in the spring.

• Or take cuttings from the sweet potato vine in the fall, just before the first frost. Cut 6–8" of top growth from the plant, place it in a glass of water and set in a sunny place. When the cutting produces roots, plant in a pot. It makes a great houseplant.

You don't have string to tie plants

• Carry wide, dental floss in your pocket for this purpose. It's convenient and very strong. It's also handy if you get something caught in your teeth.

The trellis plant stops blooming

• Plant "trellis buddies," two plants that can coexist and will bloom in sequence. For example, everblooming 10' "Climbing Ramblin' Red" shrub roses (an improved "Henry Kelsey") and *Clematis terniflora* "Sweet Autumn" will flower from June to frost. The clematis has clusters of starry white flowers that bloom as long as two months in the fall and perfume the entire garden with a heavenly sweet fragrance. Both are hardy to zone 3.

• Another plant that looks beautiful growing with a clematis is bridal wreath Spirea. Let the clematis twine through the bush. Try the new disease-resistant variety, *Spiraea vanhouttei* "Renaissance." From a single plant to a hedge that can grow to 7' (and makes a wonderful privacy barrier), the arching branches of bridal wreath make it a beautiful addition to the landscape. Plant blue-flowered small spring bulbs such as grape hyacinths around the base of the shrub.

The vines won't climb a post

• Twist a few lengths of grapevine, from prunings or from a wreath, into a spiral from the bottom of the post to the top. Attach it with wire. The grapevine is more attractive than wire and string, and it looks more natural.

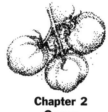

Chapter 2
Crops

TOMATOES

Don't You Hate It When...

You have no garden space to plant tomatoes

• Purchase Topsy Turvy™, a hanging bag that lets you grow upside-down tomatoes in limited areas. Even if you have space, growing upside-down tomatoes is fun. (And you can pick them right side up.)

• Or make your own hanging tomato container: To a post or wall in a sunny place, attach a sturdy hook at least 6' high. You'll need a 5-gallon bucket (which you can paint to match your house with Krylon® plastic spray paint). Drill a 1½" hole in the center of the bottom of the bucket plus four or five smaller holes for drainage. Take a tomato plant, turn it upside down into the 5-gallon pot, and carefully push its stem through the large hole so that the top end hangs out the bottom. Wrap a strip from a clean cotton towel around the base of the tomato stem that remains inside the pot so it won't fall out the hole. Fill the bucket with good potting soil, plant herbs like parsley, basil or oregano, and hang it from the pole hook. Water and fertilize regularly and before long you will be picking fresh tomatoes from the bottom and herbs from the top.

You can't remember which tomato plant is which

• Attach labels to the tops of tomato supports to identify the plant when it's full-grown.

You don't know which kind of tomato to plant

• Want to can tomatoes or make salsa? Then plant determinate tomatoes, which produce a crop that's ready to be picked all at once. "Patio," a robust plant that grows less that 3½' tall, is widely available; "Hartland," a new variety, produces more and better-tasting fruit. Determinates are shorter and don't need as much staking.

• Want quality fruit that ripens on the vine? Choose indeterminate tomatoes. Once they start to bear fruit, they'll continue to produce top growth and more fruit as long as night temperatures are warm, and they will grow for years in a frost-free environment. "Early Girl" and "Big Early" are early ripeners. "Super Fantastic" is a mid-season tomato. "Big Boy" "Better Boy," and "Brandywine" are late tomatoes. "Brandywine" has low production but exceptional flavor.

• Want a summer-long harvest and a plant that grows so slowly you don't have to build a structure to support it? Then try semi-determinates, such as "Long Keeper," "Celebrity," "Husky Red," and "Husky Gold." The "Long Keeper" has been bred to be picked in fall and ripen in winter. It doesn't taste like a vine-ripened tomato but it's better than what you'll get at the supermarket.

Tomato plants grow slowly

• Tomatoes don't like being cold. If its root ball is planted too deep in the early spring, it may stop growing, and the plant may send out new roots closer to the surface. This plan gets the plant off to a great start by keeping the root ball warm from the beginning: Buy the tallest plant you can find and remove all but the top four sets of leaves. Dig a 3" trench that runs north and south. Lay the plant in the trench with the root ball on the south end and bend the tip with its four leaves so it's above ground. Then fill in the trench, covering the plant except for the tip. Place a stake on the north side of the tip of the tomato for support. Use a starter fertilizer or fish emulsion (see page 124 for Dramm's fish emulsion) to get it off to a good start. The buried stem will sprout roots, and a bigger root system produces more fruit.

It's too cool to grow tomatoes and peppers

• Dig a hole in the sunniest spot in the garden, then halfway bury a big black nursery pot. (The perfect sized pot is used for potted trees.) Fill it with good loamy soil that includes compost and well-rotted manure. The above ground portion will absorb solar energy to heat the soil. When the soil reaches 60° F (test it with a soil thermometer), plant one tomato per pot and 2 to 3 peppers per 5-gallon pot. The pot will keep the soil warm, which will help the plants bear fruit. If the temperature drops below 60° F at night, place a cardboard box over the plant. Give the plant a low nitrogen fertilizer over the summer and keep the soil moist. This method also works for okra.

• Or jump-start your tomatoes: Use the teepee-shaped Wall O' Water®. Since it lets you put out plants 6–8 weeks ahead of schedule, you'll have an earlier harvest. Water-filled plastic tubes encircle the plant, absorb solar heat by day and release it by night. This protects tomatoes, egg-plant, peppers, squash, and melons.

• Or make your own version:

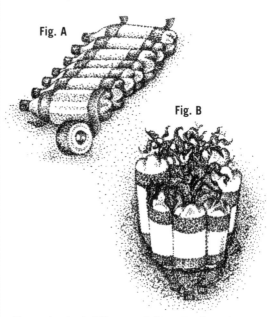

Fig. A

Fig. B

For each plant, fill seven 2-liter plastic soda bottles with water and replace the caps. Line the bottles up on their sides (all facing one direction, necks up). With long lengths of clear duct tape, tape together the top of the bottles, then the bottoms. The idea is to make a strip of connected bottles. After the tomato is planted, encircle the plant with the seven connected bottles. Then push the bottles, cap end down, into the soil just far enough so they are stabilized. Make sure the bottles are standing securely, and use duct tape to close up the circle. The water will keep the tomatoes warm by absorbing solar heat by day and releasing it at night. Put a clear plastic bag over the bottles to make it act like a mini-greenhouse (but on warm spring days, remove the plastic bag; replace it when it gets chilly again).

• One more: Make a compost hole and fill it with mown clippings from early spring growth (provided your lawn hasn't been treated with pesticides or pre-emergents), then put a plant on top. The compost hole will heat up much faster than soil and spur the plant to grow. For each plant, dig a hole 2' deep and 2' in diameter, and dump in a generous amount of clippings—up to half a bushel or so. Place a hollow pipe to one side of the hole, one end down among the clippings and the other above ground to expel any gas buildup. (Without the pipe, there would be no air flow and the grass would rot, not decompose.) Cover the clippings with 6–8" of garden soil, and then plant the plant over the compost hole. As the clippings

2   Crops

decompose, they will create heat that warms the soil and helps the plants to root. The roots will feed on the nutrients in the decomposing clippings. This tip can be used for peppers, squash, and melons, too.

Tomato stakes don't do the job

• Build a sturdy, free-standing trellis to support tomatoes. Buy three 4x4 cedar posts (not pressure-treated wood in a vegetable garden) and three Post Ups™ to hold them (they look like giant tent stakes, have clamps to hold the posts, and eliminate the need to dig post holes). You also need four 8' 2x4 crosspieces. Set the Post Ups™ so the distance between the inside edges is 8', drive them into the ground and put the posts in them. Then hang the cross-pieces (two on each side of the middle post), securing them to all three posts with L-shaped brackets. Attach lattice to the 2x4's.

Conventional ties damage staked tomatoes

• Use pantyhose. Cut off the legs and then cut them into 1" horizontal strips.

Wires from the growing cage cut into tomato stems

• Buy ½" water-pipe foam insulation tubes and fit them over the cage to cushion the plant stems. Secure the tubes with duct tape to the tomato hoop. Tomatoes will grow to maximum size.

Tomatoes start rotting on the vine

• Tomatoes rot when they can't take up calcium. To prevent this problem, add gypsum in the spring before planting, avoid high-nitrogen fertil-izers, and keep plants constantly supplied with water. (Plants that are stressed by going from wet to dry are more likely to develop this condition.)

• Pot-grown tomatoes are more vulnerable to blossom end rot than those grown in the ground.

The best way to prevent the problem is to plant the tomatoes in large pots, water them regularly, and add gypsum, extra perlite, and compost to the potting soil.

• Whiskey barrels are perfect pots for tomatoes because they're large, inexpensive, and dark (so they collect solar heat that warms the soil).

Mike's Pick:
Hardiest Tomato Plant

• **The new beefsteak tomato, "Big Beef" is an all-American selection winner. It's got hybrid vigor and is very disease resistant. The fruit can weigh up to a pound and it matures 73 days after being put into the garden. It's also great-tasting.**

Tomatoes have to be picked before they're ripe

Here are four ways to ripen green tomatoes.

• Harvest fruits that are larger than half-grown. Remove the stem, loosely wrap the tomato in newspaper, and set them in a shallow box in one loosely packed layer, stem side down, in a cool dark place. Tear back some of the paper to check the fruit and discard any that become wrinkled or spoiled.

• In early September, prune away any stems that don't have maturing fruit. Wherever you see a tomato that is half the size of the mature fruit, cut the stem just above it. The plant will put its energy into ripening the fruit rather than producing more green tomatoes.

• Before the first frost, prune stems that don't have fruit that is at least half-grown (smaller fruit won't ripen). Then uproot the plant, take it to a dry, dark place (like a garage) and hang it upside down from a rafter. Put a basket under the plant to catch any tomatoes that may fall between inspections. Most of the large tomatoes will ripen and taste like a normally vine-ripened tomato.

• Another trick to ripening tomatoes requires a garden fork. Push it into the soil at the base of the tomato and move it around just enough to loosen up the root system without uprooting the plant. The idea is to stress the plant so it will go into survival mode and try to produce as many seeds as possible before it dies; thus it will ripen its fruit quickly so that the seeds will survive.

Hot weather ruins your lettuce crop

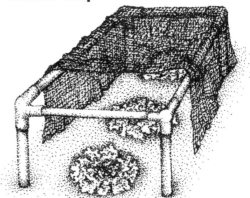

• Lettuce likes cool weather, but you can extend its growing season by shading it. Make a lettuce cover in any size you need with PVC pipe and fittings, covered with Reemay®, a light spun cloth, or cheesecloth. Available at garden centers.

• Or cover the area with garden chairs.

You have very limited space for your vegetable garden

• Adopt the clever technique Native Americans used for centuries and plant "the three sisters"— corn, pole beans, and squash—in the same plot. The corn stands tall and provides support for the pole beans to climb. The pole beans fix (or in layman's term, add) nitrogen which the corn needs to grow.

Squash vines cover the ground, keeping down weeds and providing shade so soil stays cool and ground stays moist.

You don't know when the soil is ready for beans, corn, squash, and cucumber.

• A good soil thermometer will tell you when the soil is right—60° F—but so will your feet. If you can walk comfortably on the soil with your bare feet, these heat-loving seeds can be planted. Get three harvests by planting three separate crops of corns and beans, each two weeks apart.

Harvesting leaves open patches in the garden

• Plant the next crop of vegetables in the patches. Where peas grew, you can raise a fall crop of broccoli, kale, or kohlrabi. Direct sow these plants in July, adding a little garden lime to keep them healthy. Or plant the broccoli, kale, and kohlrabi in spring and replace them with peas at the end of August.

• Radishes, lettuce, scallions, and spinach can be planted in a bare garden spot as late as September.

Certain crops are always thirsty

• Melons, tomatoes, squash, and cucumber need slow, deep watering. Before setting out the seedlings or sowing the seeds, make a water reservoir with a 5-pound coffee can. Punch just three or four tiny holes in the can, then fill the can with water, and see how long it takes to drain—ideally two or more hours. If it drains too slowly, punch in a few more holes, but be aware that it will drain more slowly when it's in the ground. Once you are happy with the drip rate, bury the can, leaving only an inch above ground. Place the lid on the can. Fill the can when plants need extra water and repeat as often as possible.

• Cucumbers are planted by threes and fours in hills, so incorporate a drip can in the hill (with holes punched all around the can) and plant around it.

• Tomatoes are planted individually and need water to go directly to their roots. Punch holes only on the side of the drip can that faces the tomato.

• If a garden has no access to water and a hose, use the same system with a 5-gallon bucket. But leave only a third of the bucket below ground and make sure all the holes are below that level. Be sure to replace the lid so you don't find critters making themselves at home in the can or bucket.

Your crops are sparse

• Increase your harvest by using a natural plant hormone, like Bonide® Tomato & Blossom Set spray. It encourages the plant to produce more flowers and fruit. Spray the flowers and adjacent leaves every week or two to promote fruiting.

You don't have enough sun to grow vegetables

• As few as three to four hours of sun are enough to grow some vegetables. You'll have success with leafy greens and root vegetables, especially the lighter-colored ones, but not with vegetables that are seeds or hold their seed (such as corn, tomatoes, peas, and beans). They'll need twice as much room as if they were planted in full sun, and they'll look different from crops that are grown in a full-sun garden, but you'll get some results.

You can't grow Bermuda onions

• If you're gardening in a northern climate, instead grow Spanish onions. They're available as green scallions, seedlings, or bulblets. Scallions and seedlings will not form as big an onion but they'll keep longer.

• To grow the largest onions possible, keep the ground moist and use a fertilizer that's high in nitrogen.

Your onions are growing slowly

• Don't cover grown onion bulbs with soil. It slows down the growth of the bulb. Just tuck them in, leaving half of the bulb above ground.

You don't know how to harvest onions

• As onions mature, the stems tend to fall over just above the bulb. When the stems of half the crop have fallen, kick over the remainder. Leave the onion bulbs in the ground for two weeks, then gather and store them in a cool, dry place.

You can't grow garlic from cloves in the supermarket

• You have to use organic garlic cloves from co-ops or mail order (irish-eyes.com is a good source), and start them this summer so they will be ready next year. In mid-August, plant the

cloves in rows, 12" apart, then fertilize them.
By the end of September, the plants should be
3–4" high. When the ground starts to freeze,
cover the plants with straw or oak leaves. Then
uncover and top dress with compost or manure
in the spring. Water throughout the summer
and watch for the bud, a mass of tiny bulbs
that look like a flower head. Remove it (it's
edible) so that the garlic puts its energy into
the bulb. By mid July the garlic will be mature
and the stems dry. Dig the bulbs and set them
in a cool, dry place. Restart the cycle by taking
the largest bulb you harvested and planting
the individual cloves in mid-August.

Your pea crop is sparse and weak

• Though most seed packages say to plant peas
from $1\frac{1}{2}$–2" deep, if you plant them 6" deep,
you'll get more pea pods and sturdier plants
with a heavier stem. The roots of deeply planted peas will be in cooler soil, which they prefer.

Peas sprout late

• In the fall make a trench running east and
west, then pile the soil on the north side of the
row. In the spring, when the soil from the ridge
has thawed, plant the peas in the bottom of
the trench, and push the soil over them. Now

peas will sprout early, with cool temperatures of spring. (If you plant radishes in a row 3" to the south of the peas, the two will grow together and can be harvested even before you plant other crops like tomatoes and cucumbers.)

Potato crop is sparse

• To make the potatoes larger and more abundant, pick off any buds you see so the plant's energy isn't diverted into producing flowers.

There are lots of weeds in the potato patch

• After potatoes have emerged, cut comfrey stems and mulch the ground around the plants. Comfrey will keep weeds down, help retain moisture in the soil, and provide nitrogen and potassium to the potatoes.

Squash and melons rot

• Keep squash and melons off the ground when they are growing. Use coffee cans with lids as perches for the young fruit, which can remain there until maturity.

• You can even use pantyhose to make a sling for melons. (Gosh. I wonder how someone came up with that idea.)

• Or set melons and squash on broken pieces of concrete or flat stepping stones. Because the stones trap heat, they'll also help your crops ripen more quickly.

Garden vegetables are hard to clean

• Gather them in a plastic laundry basket or plastic milk crate and rinse off the dirt with a garden hose. Drain the produce before bringing it indoors.

• Sturdy vegetables can be cleaned in the washing machine. Use cold water and a gentle cycle. But don't put them in the dryer.

There's no room to grow strawberries

• Attach a length of gutter that is enclosed at each end to a fence, on patio railings or on a garden wall. Fill it with potting soil and you have the perfect container to grow strawberries. They have a short root system and will look pretty as they hang. In some climates, you'll have to bury the gutters in the fall to protect the strawberries. Put them in empty space in the garden or the compost pile. In the spring, hang them back up.

You aren't sure about prime eating time for your crops

• Vegetables that must be picked and eaten once they're ready to harvest include beans (they'll get woody on the vine), corn (it loses sugar content), cucumbers (which develop seeds in the core), and peas (which lose vitamins and sugar, so they're less tender).

• Vegetables that can wait up to a week past peak harvest time without losing flavor or vitamins include broccoli, cabbage, cauliflower, kohlrabi, lettuce, okra, radish, summer squash, tomatillo, and tomatoes.

• Vegetables that can wait for several weeks past prime harvest time without losing flavor or quality include root crops such as beets, carrots, potatoes, and turnips, plus garlic, kale, leeks, onions, pumpkins, shell beans, and winter squash.

Mike's Pick:
The Best Carrot

• **Thumbelina, an All-American Selection winner, is short, almost round, with great flavor. It matures in about 60 days and is a good choice if you have poor or rocky soil.**

Chapter 3
Lawns, Shrubs,
and Trees

LAWNS

Don't You Hate It When...

You're not sure when the spring lawn or garden can be walked on

• Step on it. If a print is visible when you lift your foot, the lawn is still too wet to walk on. Do the step test every few days. Once a foot-print no longer remains, the lawn is ready for traffic.

• Don't work in the garden in the early spring. Walking on wet garden soil compacts it. Test the soil for wetness by taking a small sample and squeezing it into a ball. If it stays in a ball when you open your hand, it may be too wet. If you can crumble it up, then you can work in the garden.

Grass doesn't grow fast enough

• Put grass seed in the freezer for 24 hours before you sow it, and cut the germination time in half. The seed will be "tricked" into believing it went through a dormant winter period. Those bare spots will be green in no time.

You're not sure when to seed a lawn

• The best time to seed a lawn is in the fall (from the end of August through mid-September). The second-best time is early spring (from mid-April to early May).

You can't broadcast grass seeds evenly

• Poke holes in the bottom of an empty coffee can with an ice pick or hammer and nail to make an ideal dispenser. Pour in the seed, cover the can with its lid, and shake the dispenser over the area to be seeded. If the holes aren't big enough, enlarge them with a screwdriver or a larger nail.

Grass seed washes away or is eaten by birds

• Reseed bare spots, then use cheesecloth as mulch. It doesn't contain any weed seeds and it lets the sunshine in. Stake the edges with small wooden stakes or fabric staples. The new grass will grow under the cheesecloth easily. Remove the cheesecloth when the grass needs mowing.

Brown patches appear on the lawn

• When dogs or disease cause spots in the summer lawn, instead of planting seed, make a patch. With a flat spade, cut the damaged spot (square or rectangular cuts are easiest to deal with), then remove it along with 3" of soil. Find a lightly trafficked spot, cut out a similarly shaped piece of sod and transfer it to the prepared hole, watering it well. Keep the patch moist and soon it will blend in seamlessly. In the fall, reseed the area where you harvested the patches.

• Or to patch your lawn, remove the dead grass and then loosen soil to a depth of 3". Sprinkle grass seeds, about 4–6 per inch. (Remember, each seed is not a single blade, but a whole plant.) Cover the surface with ½" of peat moss. Water enough to keep the moss a bark-brown color. (Peat moss is dark brown when wet and light brown when dry).

• For large lawns, have an area where sod patches can be harvested when needed.

Steep slopes of your lawn develop bare spots

• Grass seed on slopes usually washes away before it germinates. To fill the patches, plant grass seed in a seedling flat. In a few weeks you'll have a tray of healthy grass to transplant as needed. Secure with garden staples. (They look like giant paper staples and are meant to hold landscape sod, fabric, and plastic in place.) Or make your own with wire coat hangers that are cut and bent into U-shaped staples.

Dog urine and road salt damages your lawn (and garden)

• Pelletized gypsum is a must for every garden. It not only repairs damage caused by dog urine and road salts, but also encourages deep root growth that creates strong, healthy grass and plants by supplying calcium and sulfur, and it counteracts alkaline soils high in sodium. Water thoroughly after applying. Amounts to use:

- For general application, 40 pounds per 1000 square feet of turf or garden.

- For established trees, shrubs, and ever greens, 2 cups at the drip-line.

- In compost, 4 cups for each wheelbarrow of material and 2 cups each time the pile is turned.

- To prevent road salt damage, in fall apply 40 pounds per 100 square feet of turf.

Mushrooms grow in the lawn

• Lawn mushrooms are the fruiting bodies of a fungus that lives off organic matter in the soil. You can only mow them down. When the weather changes; the mushrooms will stop coming up.

You don't know what to do with sod you've removed

• Instead of lugging heavy sod away, make a new garden. Just turn it over in a new bed and compost it down.

Grass is diseased and dying

• You may have used too much seed. More lawn seed is not better, since each seed produces not a single blade but an actual grass plant that requires space to grow. If you have put down too many seeds, the small seedlings will compete for space and choke one another out, resulting in diseased and dying grass; and you'll spend seed money unnecessarily. You need only four to six seeds per square inch of ground to produce a healthy lawn.

Mike's Pick:
Best Organic Lawn Weed Control and Fertilizer

• Renaissance® 10-0-0, made with a corn byproduct. Corn gluten kills sprouting weeds before they become a problem.

The grass is greener at your neighbor's place

• In the spring, spread ½" of compost over the entire surface of your lawn, and then use the back of the rake to level it. Wait a month, and then apply another ½" of compost. In the fall, apply another layer before sowing grass seed.

Dry weather kills the lawn

• You can help lawns survive drought periods by setting the mower high, at 3". Taller grass will shade the soil, conserve water, and prevent weed seed from germinating. (Fewer weeds mean more moisture for the grass.) Cut the lawn often at this height so the grasses won't lie down, and make sure the blade is sharp enough to cut the grass rather than rip it.

You're not sure when to go after lawn weeds

• Do it in spring or fall. In spring, when broadleaf weeds (like dandelion and plantains) are ready to bloom, they're putting energy into blooming and the herbicide catches them off guard. In the heat of summer, most weeds have developed a thicker leaf and are less likely to die after one application. In fall, after the first or second frost, many perennial weeds move energy down into the root system. When you spray, the herbicide will be drawn deep inside.

• The best time to spot weeds is when you're mowing. Slip a flour-filled mustard or ketchup squeeze bottle into your pocket before you start. When you're mowing and see a weed, squeeze a bit of flour on it as a marker so it'll be easy to find later on.

SHRUBS

Azaleas aren't thriving

• Coffee grounds might help. Starbucks® offers packaged used coffee grounds—free! That's a great excuse for a gardener to feed a latte habit.

• Azaleas love oak leaves, too. Use them as mulch around each bush.

You can't grow oleander in the north

• Large oleander shrubs in southern gardens come in red and many shades of pink and white, but they can also be enjoyed in the north as tropical container plants. In the spring when night temperatures average about 50° F, the plants can be moved outside and placed in a sunny spot. Keep oleander on the dry side and use a low nitrogen fertilizer. Oleanders will bloom all summer if temperatures are warm to hot. As flowers fade, remove them to encourage more bloom. In the fall you can cut back as much as one-third of the plant, but cutting back isn't necessary if it's of manageable size.

Overgrown lilac shrubs are out of control

• Lilacs can grow to a height of 15' and width of 12' wide. To get control over a plant that size without cutting it down to the ground will take three seasons. In the fall cut off one-third of the largest canes all the way to the ground. This will reduce the size of the plant and let smaller branches get light. Repeat for two subsequent falls, and you'll get a smaller shrub that can be lightly sheared after flowering.

Spring shrubs have stopped blooming

• Plant clematis on the shady side of a small tree or large shrub, like viburnum or lilac and let the vine do what nature intended. The clematis will grow up through the plant and bloom on the top. This doesn't hurt the shrub or the vine, and the clematis will bloom after the shrub has stopped.

Mike's Pick:
Best Way to Protect Evergreens

• **Wilt-Pruf® is an anti transpirant. Spray it on all evergreens, holly, and boxwoods in the fall to prevent moisture loss. Also, spray it on cut Christmas trees, treetops, and other greens to keep them fresh. And in the event of drought, spray it on plants in spring and summer. For more information, check out wiltpruf.com.**

Yews turn brown in the winter

• Yews, rhododendrons, and Alberta spruce, particularly in south and west locations, are subject to winter burn when sun and wind dry them out. To avoid the problem, make sure the soil is wet in the fall and remains wet going into freezing. If your soil doesn't freeze, keep it moist all winter.

• And make a protective screen for the plant. Build a teepee around it with garden stakes, wrap burlap over the frame and secure it with string or staples so the material remains in place all winter. But if you're not especially fond of a landscape that includes burlap teepees, use Wilt-Pruf® in the fall. Like thin, white glue that dries clear, it seals the leaves so they don't dry out over the winter (but you must keep the ground moist before it freezes).

TREES

Trees are messy with branches that are weak and break easily

• The fastest-growing trees usually produce the most debris, with branches that break easily in a storm. But, oak trees (a sturdy, clean tree) contrary to myth, grow relatively quickly when young. The new English oak crossbreeds, like *Quercus x macdanielli* "Heritage" and *Quercus x warei* "Regal Prince," are especially fast growing.

Mike's Pick:
Hardiest Shade Tree

• Ginkgo trees grow slowly but mature beautifully. They're virtually disease- and insect-free, tolerate a wide range of soil conditions, and can be planted almost anywhere. The fan-shaped leaf is a pleasant green in the summer, bright gold in fall. When they drop to the ground overnight in autumn, they create a carpet of gold that is easy to rake. Buy a male so you don't have to worry about the messy fruit.

Young maples and other trees get sun scale

• Sun scale is caused during winter, when sun heats the bark of the tree by day and the temperatures drop at night. That damages the bark so that cracks appear in the spring. You can prevent the problem by wrapping young trees with cardboard. The young tree has a small diameter, so you might be able to slit a couple of gift wrapping paper tubes up one side and manage to cover the entire diameter with just two of them, or perhaps you can find a mailing tube large enough for your purpose. You have to cover the entire trunk, all the way up to the first branch.

• Or protect the tree with lengths of 1½" diameter plastic swimming-pool hose, the kind used to vacuum the pool. Use a utility knife to cut the hose a length equal to the distance between the ground and the first branch. Then cut vertically and snap the hose around the tree truck.

You don't know how to choose evergreens

• Choose one that fits the space. Don't buy one you'll have to prune, and look for a dwarf version if the one you like grows too big.

• The most popular evergreens are pine, spruce, and fir, since they grow quickly and are inexpensive.

• Larch, hemlock, and cedar are excellent additions if the spot is suitable. Larch likes moist soil, hemlock prefers shade, and cedar is excellent for hedging.

• For any large garden space, consider fast-growing Norway spruce. It grows to 80' high and 30' across, and has horizontal spreading branches that develop pendulous branchlets.

• The Scotch pine, the classic Christmas tree, grows quickly up to 60' high and an umbrella-shaped 40' wide. It can be trained as if it were growing on a wind-swept coast, as if it were high on a mountain, or in many other ways. Anything cut from the young tree will just give it more shape and character; but if never pruned, it will develop a personality of its own. The unique orange-brown coloration on the upper bark is very attractive in the winter months.

• Spruce look their best when small and medium but tend to develop diseases once they are 20 years old and should be cut down then (though they can live another decade and even more.) Make sure to replace it with another tree that is appropriate to the space.

A row of evergreens is of different sizes and crowded

• When planting a row of evergreens, it's very important to plant them at the same time and space them the recommended distance apart or they'll look crowded. (And they might fight with each other.)

Blue spruce trees look unattractive as they grow

• Young blue spruces have been pruned by the nursery. But they won't keep that shape without pruning unless they are one of the named varieties, such as "Fat Albert," which has a powdery blue color and a uniform growth habit. Named varieties aren't grown from seed but are grafted onto a root stock. This makes them more expensive, but the difference in price is worth it.

• Or consider "Swiss Stone" which looks like white pine and has long, soft, blue-tinted needles. A dense slow-growing evergreen that gets as high as 40' and wide as 20', it's disease- and insect-free, keeps its lower branches as long as there is sunlight, and can be grown as far north as zone 2. Somewhat hard to find and possibly costly (because it's slow-growing), it's worth seeking out. Give it plenty of room so that the bottom branches can be maintained right down to the ground.

• If you have limited room, choose "Silver Whispers" which is only 12' high and 6' wide.

Arborvitae bends in the middle during the winter

• These tall evergreens, often with multiple trunks that form their pyramid shape, may suf- fer when a layer of heavy snow or thick ice bends their branches. Shaking off the snow might damage the tree. Wait for the snow and ice to melt and the tree will try to grow straight again.

• Or, as a protective measure, wrap the tree snugly with black plastic netting made to keep birds away from fruit trees. It will keep the stems of the arborvitae together and is almost invisible. In the spring remove the netting and save it for next year.

There are no tall trees on your property

• Spading is a new technique for moving large trees to a new site to make a landscape look mature. It works reasonably well for deciduous trees with a trunk diameter of less than 7" or for evergreens less than 10' tall. But moving larger evergreens (up to 20') is problematic. (See page 63, "You can't save an established tree.") Even if the operator is skilled and the soil is compatible, big trees tend to drop a lot of needles from the stress of the move and may stay sparse for up to a decade or even die in a few seasons.

• Whenever you contract for spaded evergreen or deciduous trees, get a guarantee that sick-looking or dead trees will be replaced. Otherwise, you're better off planting smaller balled-and-burlapped trees that come with a warranty. In a transplant situation, some trees may die and must be replaced. You will find that new, smaller trees will often grow as big as the transplants in very few seasons, since the stress of a move often slows the trans-plants' growth rate.

• If you have a tree removed, have the trunk cut into various lengths, from 1–3'. Set them in your garden with potted plants on top to add elevation and variety.

You can't save an established tree

• Good news! A large tree can be moved if the job isn't rushed. If you want to save an established tree, you will have to prepare it at least six months and preferably a year before the move. Once it's prepared, it can be moved in spring or fall, depending on when the roots were cut.

1. Determine the proper size of the root ball. For every inch of the tree diameter, go out 6" from the base; so for a 3" trunk, measure out 18" for the root ball on each of four sides of the tree and place a stake to mark the spot. Run a piece of twine between the stakes.

2. In the spring dig a 2' deep trench from one stake to another and a parallel trench on the opposite side. Refill the trenches with compost or quality top soil.

3. In the fall dig trenches on the remaining two sides. Now the tree has been root pruned. Again refill the trenches with compost or quality top soil.

4. Dig up the tree and move it to its new home before the plant comes out of its dormant state in spring or after it goes dormant in the fall.

• Note: To move a shrub or small tree, follow steps 1 and 2 shown above. Let set for two weeks before the shrub is moved to its new location. By this time, new roots will have started developing.

You have to kill a tree stump

• Even after a deciduous tree is cut down, the roots remain alive and send out shoots. To prevent them from growing, use several unopened black plastic bags as sheets to cover the stump. Be sure to cover the area where the trunk meets the roots so no light can come through, and secure the bags with rocks and string or a bungee cord. If you cover a stump in the fall, shoots will stop growing and the stump will be ready to remove by late spring.

• Unless a stump is ground down with professional equipment, it will take time to remove completely. A large stump needs to be aged for at least 18 months and treated with a herbicide so it won't sprout. Then use Bonide® Stump Out™, following the directions. In about three months the stump should be gone. Exactly how long it will take to remove the stump will be determined by the size and type of the tree involved. (Bonide® isn't effective on a green stump.)

An old stump can't be removed

• Convert it into a planter. Drill out the center of the stump and fill with potting soil for flowers.

Salt spray from snow removal kills roadside trees and shrubs

• Your best offense is a good defense. Put plants that will tolerate salt spray near the road. Ask your local garden center.

You don't know where to prune a limb

• Look closely at where the branch meets the trunk of the tree and you'll see a raised ring around the branch. It's called the branch collar. Prune so that the branch collar is cut, and don't leave a stub. The cut will heal faster with an intact collar, and a stub is susceptible to rot that will enter the main trunk.

You can't mow the lawn because the tree branches are too low

• When a young tree is planted, the lower branches need to be pruned as the tree grows. You don't want those branches to get too big before you remove them because it's hard on the tree to lose major branches. Over the course of three to four seasons, remove lower branches of the young tree. Take one or two of the lowest branches off at a time. The goal is to have the branching start at about 6'–7' above the ground. If you prune, do it during the winter months when the tree is dormant. Once you have the branching pattern that you want, remove small side branches off the main branch system. This will help create a beautiful tree.

The leaves on your trees have raised bumps

• Whether there are many or a few, whether they're the size of a pinhead or a marble, they're caused by insects such as tiny wasps or mites. Unfortunately, spraying for these creatures is virtually impossible, so nothing can be done about them. However, they're not detrimental to the tree.

Chapter 4
Root Cuttings, Seeds,
and Seedlings

ROOT CUTTINGS

Don't You Hate It When...

Root cuttings don't grow

• If you want to root soft and semi-soft plants, put them in willow water. It's the best way to help establish new roots, since it contains a hormone that stimulates root growth. To make a small quantity of willow water in which to place your cuttings, cut one or two small-diameter willow stems about 6" long from wood less than three years old. (The smaller the diameter of the willow stem, the more hormone it will contain.) Strip off the leaves, place the stems in a glass of water, then add your plant cuttings. Let them soak overnight.

• To speed root formation once the root cutting is planted in soil (geraniums, for example), water the soil with willow water. Remove the leaves from a handful of fresh willow twigs and place them in a gallon of warm water for 24 hours. Then remove the twigs, and use the water in your watering can. Any unused portion will stay good for a week if refrigerated. Make up fresh batches as needed, but the sooner you use willow water the more effective it is. (Note: Fresh willow can be bought from most florists year round.)

Root cuttings rot when transplanted to potting soil

• If your cuttings develop a few fine roots but you've had bad luck planting them directly into potting soil, try transplanting them into moist vermiculite. It's a sterile product that allows roots that have started in water to get used to heavier soils. Once the plant has developed a strong root ball in the vermiculite, transplant it into good quality potting soil. The plant should establish itself quickly.

SEEDS

You don't know how to store leftover seeds

• Store leftover seeds in a tightly sealed jar in a cool, dry place. Tuck in a slip of paper that identifies the name of the plant and its cultivation requirements. Also add 2 tablespoons of powdered milk wrapped in two layers of tissue, which will keep the seed dry. The extended storage time reduces the likelihood that a seed will come up, so expect a lower-than-normal germination rate.

• Or store them in plastic sheets designed to hold trading cards. Keep the sheets in a wide-spine, three-ring binder. And make sure the

kids don't get confused and carry them off to a baseball card convention.

• Or, when planting time arrives, string a clothesline across the inside of the garage and use clothespins to attach the seed packets. I betcha you'll remember they're there.

Seed starting equipment is too expensive

• Save your money, and instead use Styrofoam® containers, the kind in which mushrooms and cherry tomatoes are packed. They're the perfect size to start a package of seeds. When the seedlings are large enough, transplant them into Styrofoam® coffee cups. Be sure to poke a drain hole in the bottom of all containers.

• Or use cardboard toilet paper rolls as seed-starting pots. Cut them in half and place them onto a metal baking sheet, which conducts heat efficiently if you place it on a seed-start-ing mat. Fill the cardboard halves with potting mix, and plant the seeds. When the seedlings are ready to be transplanted, slide them into the ground by pushing the tubes partway into the soil but leaving the upper parts of the tubes sticking up above the soil line. The upper tubing provides some protection for the seedlings, and the lower portion will protect the plant from cutworms. The tubes will decompose. Make sure the seedlings are hardened gradually before transplanting.

Potting soil makes a mess when filling pots

• Instead of a potting bench, buy a large black polystyrene tub. Use it as a tray when filling pots with soil. Line up the pots in the tub and pour soil from the bag into them. The tub catches the soil and you save time cleaning. Look for large tubs at farm supply and automotive stores.

Planting tiny seeds is difficult

• Place a layer of toilet paper on the soil, then sprinkle the seeds over the toilet paper. You'll be able to see exactly where the seeds land and spread them evenly. Then sprinkle a thin layer of potting mix over the seeds and water them. The seeds will sprout through the toilet paper, which eventually will dissolve.

• Another solution for tiny seeds, like poppy seeds, is to mix them with four parts sand and sow them with a glass grated-cheese dispenser, the old-fashioned kind with a metal lid and large holes.

71

Seeds don't sprout

• Start seeds in 6" squares of dark corduroy fabric (preferably cut from those old worn-out pants your spouse just kept hanging onto). Begin by wetting the corduroy, then wringing it out. Sprinkle the seeds on the smooth side of the cloth, fold the cloth over and run it under water so the seeds are thoroughly soaked. Lightly press out the water, and place the folded squares in a large plastic container with a lid. Check the seeds occasionally. When they begin to sprout, plant them in a professional seed starter mix.

There's no place to start seeds indoors

• A covered plastic sweater box makes a perfect mini-greenhouse. Turn the lip upside down and place the seed flats on top of it. Then cover the lid with the box itself, and don't remove it until the seeds germinate. You will probably need to water it only once.

You don't have a greenhouse to start seeds outdoors

• Make mini greenhouses with 2-liter, clear plastic soda bottles. Cut the bottom off a bottle, remove the label and cap, and punch small holes so the plant won't get too hot and bake.

Place the bottle right side up over the seedling and push it into the soil. Once a plant is tall enough to touch the top of the inside of the bottle, remove the bottle. On hot days remove the bottle cap, but put it back on before evening.

You can't keep track of where you planted larger seeds outdoors

• Use a wooden matchstick (tip side down) to mark the spot. The plants love the sulfur on the match head, too.

SEEDLINGS

Watering seedlings makes a mess

• Place your seedling pots in a tray without holes, and pour water into the tray so the seedlings can absorb the water they need from the bottom of the pots. Remove the excess with a turkey baster.

• Or cut an old bath towel into strips about 1" wide and 8–10" long. Place one end under the seedling pot. Drape the other end over the side of the plastic seedling tray and into a plastic container that is set lower than the seedling tray. The towel will wick up all the water in the bottom of the seedling flat and deposit it into the collection container, which can be emptied out.

Seedlings seem fragile

• Seedlings will develop strong, sturdy, stocky stems if you rub your hand over them every time you walk by them. (Those little pats make them grow up very secure.)

• Or use a small low-speed fan and blow air over the seedlings. It is important to move the fan so the air current changes. Start this process at any time after the seedlings have germinated, but at least two to three weeks before you plan on moving the plants outside. Note: A running fan will dry the soil so check for water needs more often.

The sun wilts newly planted seedlings

• It's best to transplant seedlings on cloudy days, but if that's impossible, arrange lawn chairs over new transplants so the seat covers them. And heck, why not sit down for a while. You'll be doing yourself and the transplants a favor.

You can't tell the difference between seedlings and weeds

• When sowing seeds directly into the garden soil, mark the planted seed with a colored toothpick or a match stick.

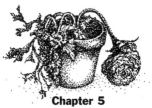

Chapter 5
Containers, Cut Flowers,
and Houseplants

CONTAINERS

Don't You Hate It When...

You don't know what to put on a sunny patio

• Tropical hibiscus *Hibiscus rosasinensis* are great patio plants. They like it hot and sunny. To keep them in bloom, use an acid fertilizer every two weeks and keep the soil evenly moist. If your water is alkaline, add one tablespoon vinegar to every gallon of water.

There's no place for a kids' garden

• Turn an old wagon into a movable garden. Drill holes in the bottom for drainage and fill it with potting soil. Move it to take advantage of morning sun and afternoon shade.

Plant containers cost a mint

• Use your imagination. Transform bathtubs, rubber boots, an old French horn, a roof vent, and anything else you can think of into a planter.

• Or do as my grandmother did, and use an old pair of shoes filled with soil and planted with moss roses and sedum. She set them by her sunny back door, and in addition to look-

ing pretty, they served an additional purpose—reminding me to take off my shoes
before coming into the house.

Potted plants are too heavy to move

• Even a large potted plant needs only 6–8" of
soil to grow in, so you needn't fill the pot with
soil. Reduce a container's weight and improve
its drainage by adding all-natural 100% hardwood charcoal to the bottom of the pot. It's
much easier to work with than packing
peanuts or soda cans.

• Or place a large nursery pot upside down on
the bottom of the pot to fill space.

Your container plants look the same year after year

• Sweet potato vine *Ipomoea batatas* grows
quickly and cascades over the edge of a container. It comes in colors that range from deep
maroon to vibrant chartreuse. The "Pink Ice"
variety has splashes of pink in the leaf.

• Licorice vine *Helichrysum* has no blooms but
does have interesting fuzzy leaves, some larger
and some compact, in silver and in chartreuse.
When they spill over the pot, the leaves add a
touch of softness.

• Silver falls *Dichondra* sends out fast-growing ropes of bright silver foliage that will be many feet long at the end of the season.

• Bushy purple knight *Alternanthera* complements most flowering plants and thrives in both sun and light shade.

• Cascading Tahitian bridal veil *Gibasis geneculata* and German ivy *Senecio mikaniodes* combine well with other shade-loving plants, flowering impatiens, and begonias.

You have to replace existing potting soil

• Potting soil, which is primarily peat moss, lacks the beneficial fungus necessary to produce healthy plants. Instead of replacing the soil, just add Myke®, a commercial product that contains mycorrhizae. Available at most garden centers or visit www.usemyke.com.

• Or purchase Oak Leaf Mold from Mosser Lee Company to accomplish the same result. Visit mosserlee.com or phone 715-284-2296.

• Or try making your own leaf mold in the fall. (Caution: it's tricky.)

1. Put dry oak leaves through a shredder or run over them with a lawn mower. They should be very finely chopped but not decayed.

Sprinkle them with just enough water to moisten them lightly, then put them in black plastic bags and place them in a sunny spot.

2. Keep the bags sealed so the leaves heat up, and turn over the bags weekly. Check inside the bag every week and if the leaves are too wet, leave it open until the leaves are moist and not wet.

3. After several weeks you'll see white mold on the leaves. This oak leaf mold can be kept outside over the winter and used in containers or in the garden in the spring.

Mike's Pick:
Best Soil for Container Plants

• Premier Horticulture makes a family of soils that work very well in containers, window boxes, and hanging baskets as well as for other applications. Premier's "Pro-Mix" combines coarse peat moss, perlite, vermiculite and limestone for drainage; a water-absorbent polymer that helps retain water; and a time-release fertilizer that feeds for nine months. Great for plants that like moisture and sunny, hot places. There's a special mix for growing edibles (vegetables and herbs). Visit www.premierhort.com or call 800-525-2553.

Relining wire baskets with moss or sphagnum annually is expensive

• Save money by using two or three layers of burlap. It's easy to cut and form into shape when wet, it doesn't dry out as quickly as moss, and it looks nice when the flowers start growing over the sides. Even if you stuff some moss over the burlap, you'll still save a bundle.

Window boxes and containers dry out constantly

• Before you fill the box with potting soil, line the base with several layers of newspaper or a not-too-thick disposable baby diaper (newborn size is ideal). Either will hold moisture so the soil won't dry out as quickly.

• If Soil Moist™ granules are added to the potting soil, you won't have to water as frequently. Soil Moist is a polymer that absorbs and releases water in soil. Follow the directions. More is not better. (Another use: Use 1 oz. per 6' row in your garden and you could reduce watering by 50%.)

• Crush floral foam and put it in a potting medium for window boxes and hanging planters. It will help the container plants retain water longer and not dry out as quickly in the wind.

Empty window boxes look so dreary in the fall

• Pull out the faded annuals and switch to fall decorations like branches of brightly colored leaves, dried grasses, seed heads, and pussy willows. To prevent them from being blown away, make a sturdy frog with rolled chicken wire. Simply cut it to make a roll that fits into the box. Squash down the top a little so it doesn't show. Replace the fall decorations with Christmas decorations in December.

You don't know what do about a root-bound plant

• When there are roots on the surface of the soil, a plant is probably root bound. (Check to see by removing the plant from the pot.) But you don't have to move it into a larger pot. Instead, take the plant from the pot, and slice away 3–4" of soil and root with a sharp knife. Add 3–4" of fresh soil to the pot, and then return the plant to the container. The plant will grow new roots in the fresh soil. Consider yourself smart for not having to buy a new, big, expensive pot.

• If you do want to move it to another pot, the pot should be at least 1" larger. Before you plant, this treatment will ensure that the plant will like its new home. Soak the root ball in

water for a few hours or overnight. Then gently tease out the outer roots that are wrapped around the root ball. Prune away any long or broken roots before planting in fresh potting soil.

A container isn't draining properly

• The best way to deal with this problem is to prevent it. Before you fill the container with soil, invert a plastic pot over the drain hole to help ensure excess water can run out.

• Be sure to put the container on feet that raise it an inch or two above the ground surface so that the area underneath can dry out between waterings. This tip has saved many decks.

CUT FLOWERS

You don't know the best way to cut flowers from the garden

• Cut them in the morning, when the dew is still on them and they are full of natural moisture.

• Use a sharp knife or Oriental shears to make a clean, sharp cut, not only on flowers but also on foliage and branches.

• Cut the stem on an angle, 1" from the end. That will expose more area to carry water to the flower blossom.

You don't know how to feed and water cut flowers

• The less time cut flowers are without water and food, the longer they will live. So take a container filled with fresh, warm, unsoftened water and commercial flower food into the garden, and plunge the flowers right into it. (Home recipes for flower food aren't effective at fighting bacteria and keeping the pH balance, which prolongs the flowers' lives. Use commercial flower food preparations from a florist or garden center.)

• Most flowers should be placed into water that is warm to the touch, but tulips, daffodils, and other bulb flowers must be placed into cool water.

• If you aren't going to arrange fresh flowers right away, put the container in a tightly sealed plastic bag before placing them in the home refrigerator or a cool basement. Otherwise, the natural gasses from fruit and vegetables may cause some petals to become transparent, foliage to turn yellow, and blossoms to fall off prematurely. Note: Don't keep them in the bag more than 12 hours.

Cut flowers have an unpleasant odor

• The strong fragrance from baby's breath can ruin a bouquet of roses. Why florists add baby's

breath to roses, I'll never know. The odor can be masked by laying the baby's breath on newspaper and spraying them with Febreze®. Then return them to the vase of water immediately.

Fresh flowers don't last

• Flowers will last longer if the vase is clean. Before washing, spray the inside of the vase with a bleach-based product, like Tilex®. Wash with warm soapy water, rinse, and let dry.

• Keep cut flowers away from extreme heat, direct sunlight, and drafts, which will dry them out. And avoid temperatures below 35° F.

• Keep fresh flowers in an open area where they can get fresh air.

• Every two days change the vase water. Remove the flowers and foliage and lay them on your work surface. Empty the vase of water, and wash, rinse, and dry it. Then place fresh warm water in the vase with the correct amount of flower food. Rinse the stems under the faucet, then cut off about 1" of each stem before returning to the vase. Some folks have told me they do this daily and their bouquet of flowers can last up to two weeks.

• Remove old and dying flowers and foliage from the arrangement. Otherwise they pollute the water with bacteria that make the remainder die more quickly.

• When daffodils are cut, they exude a sap that clogs the vessels of other flowers so they can't be properly hydrated. Place daffodils in a vase by themselves for a couple of hours before you put them with other flowers, or enjoy them alone.

Cut flowers lose their color quickly

• If foxglove is added to the bouquet, flowers will stay colorful longer.

• Or, make a foxglove infusion. Add a handful of foxglove leaves to a gallon of water and let it sit for a few days. Strain and add 2 tablespoons to each vase of fresh-cut flowers. The mixture can be stored in the refrigerator for two weeks.

Flowers and leaves fade and fall apart

• Try this easy method to dry and preserve them. Layer as many flowers and leaves as you wish in a tin (like the ones in which cookies, popcorn, or coffee is sold). Then gently pour

5 Containers, Cut Flowers, and Houseplants

cat box filler—the clumping kind—over all, and replace the lid. Thin flowers will dry in less than two weeks; thick flowers will need that long or more. Keep track of the time it takes and note it on the calendar.

• Or dry flowers with the aid of desiccants such as silica gel, borax, and sand mixtures that absorb and retain moisture. The process takes longer, but the flowers stay colorful and are high quality. Follow the directions on the package.

• Or press flowers and foliage between absorbent layers of material that draw out the moisture. You can find these in most craft centers.

• Or wrap a rubber band tightly around the stem ends of a bouquet and hang the flowers upside down in a warm, dry, dark area where air is circulated (a furnace room is ideal). The faster that the flowers dry, the more color they retain.

• Or to preserve fall leaves at the peak of their beauty, press them in layers of newspaper until they are dry. Place a sheet of white paper on your ironing board. Fold a sheet of wax paper, waxy side in, and place a tester leaf (not your favorite!) between it, colored side up. Place a second sheet of white paper over the wax paper, making a sandwich of leaves, wax paper, and white paper. With a warm iron, gently iron the paper. Check to see that the wax is melting and being absorbed by the leaf. Adjust the iron temperature and try several leaves until you get the proper effect. Additional new wax paper may be needed on a single leaf. After the waxing, put the leaves in between newspaper again and top with a heavy object, such as a book, for a day or so. Processed leaves will retain their color and natural appearance.

Dried flowers don't look good

• When dried flowers absorb moisture from the air, they break and disintegrate. Seal them by spraying them with an inexpensive firm-hold hairspray that doesn't contain oil, or ask your local hobby store for a commercial matte finish sealant made especially for dried flowers.

• To retard fading, keep dry flowers in a cool, dry room away from sunlight.

• To soften and detangle dried flowers, mist them lightly with water and store them in a sealed container for about 20 minutes. Once they are separated, gently dry the flowers with a hair dryer turned to low.

Stems are too short for the vase

• Thread floral wire through the short stem to add length.

• Or stick the stem into a clear drinking straw. Make sure the stem reaches down far enough to soak up water.

• Or float the blossoms in a bowl with floating candles or other decorative accents.

A vase of flowers isn't full enough

• Add dried flowers to the vase.

• Or add greens from the garden or houseplants.

You don't have a frog or other flower-arranging device

• Be sure the top edges of the vase are clean and dry. Using clear, waterproof anchor tape (bought from a florist) place a series of tape strips across the opening ½" apart. Then place another set of strips at right angles to the first set, so you create a grid with square openings. Secure the ends of the strips by wrapping more tape around the edge of the top of the vase.

• Or place the head of a large flower, such as a hydrangea, at the top of a vase to completely cover the opening. Push small flowers gently through the hydrangea blossom.

• Or cut fresh curly willow stems, wrap the stems around your hand, and place them into the vase in an irregular pattern. Curly willow is available at most florists.

• Or use marbles, beads, sea glass, stones, and other items as stabilizing and decorative accents. Just make sure the items are clean before you use them so you don't add bacteria to the vase.

You don't know how to work with floral foam

• Choose a container big enough to provide a good water source for the flowers and foam.

• Cut and shape the foam before wetting it.

• Put the foam into a sink of shallow water (with flower food added) and let it soak up the water. (Do not plunge it in water, which creates air pockets; flowers placed in air pockets have no water source and die quickly.) Hydrating is complete when the foam turns dark, in about a minute.

• The side that has tiny holes should face up.

• For balance in the design, place the largest, darkest flowers closest to the foam, the lightest and smallest ones further way.

• Place the flower stem into the foam by push-ing the bottom of the stem gently so it won't bend or break.

5 Containers, Cut Flowers, and Houseplants

• Once a flower is placed into the foam, don't move it at all. Pulling will cause suction between the stem end and the foam, leaving an air pocket that prevents a flower from getting water. If you want to reposition a flower, remove the stem, cut it again and place it in a new spot so it can hydrate properly.

• To add a fruit or vegetable to a foam design, first wash it. Then place two wood picks into the item about 1" apart and place the other ends of the picks into the foam. You need both picks to keep the item stabilized. Also, the wood will wick up the water, swell up, and help make the attachment to the foam more secure.

• Do not reuse foam. It contains bacteria that will shorten the life of fresh flowers.

Pollen stains your clothes

• My friend, Mary Ellen, star of *TIPical Mary Ellen*, says that this is one of the toughest stains. Don't use your hand to remove the stain, since the oil in your skin will cause the stain to penetrate into the fiber. Instead, gently remove the pollen with a chenille pipe cleaner, a soft clean cloth, or the sticky side of any tape. If a stain remains, put the affected fabric in the sun for an hour or longer.

• Or use Mary Ellen's Formula 1 stain remover on colorfast and white fabric. For more information visit www.maryellenproducts.com.

• Prevent future stains by removing the stamen—the pollen-bearing organs of a seed plant, usually composed of the anther and filament—when the flower opens.

HOUSEPLANTS

A hanging plant drips after being watered

• Cover its bottom with a shower cap for a while after you add water.

Top-heavy plants keep falling over

• Most houseplants do better when their roots are cramped into smaller spaces. So if they're falling over, don't transplant them. Just put the pot into a larger decorative pot. Fill the base with stones to give it stability and wedge Styrofoam® between the plant and the outside container.

Houseplants die when you go on vacation

• Just before you leave, water the plants well. Then place a clear plastic dry cleaning bag

over them, leaving the bag open at the base and cutting the corners off the bag to allow a little air to circulate around the plants. Your mini-greenhouse will keep your plants alive in your absence.

• Or if your bathroom receives some natural light, try this. Set plastic-coated wire racks or upside-down dish racks in your bathtub, and set potted plants (without saucers) on them. Poke shoelaces (at least two per plant) about 1" into the pot drain hole, and let the other end dangle into the tub. Run a few inches of water into the tub.

• Or commercial DriWater® will keep your plants watered when you're not there. Check your local garden center or www.driwater.com.

Houseplants bring in insects after summering outdoors

• To prevent critters from moving inside with a plant, remove any litter from the surface, hose down the plant so that the water runs out the bottom of the pot, and let the plant dry outside. Then spray the plant with horticultural oil to smother any insects that may be hiding on it, and let it dry before you take it indoors.

The water in your house disagrees with your plants

• When the tips of houseplants turn yellow and the plants drop their leaves, they may be reacting to chlorine or fluoride in the water. The simple solution is to fill the watering can and let it sit overnight before you water your plants. The chemicals will evaporate.

• Salts from the water softeners are lethal to plants. Usually only the hot water is softened, so this isn't a problem, but if your cold water is also treated, use bottled spring water on your plants.

The ideal spot for your houseplant doesn't get enough light

• Buy two of the plants that you like, and put one in the chosen spot and the other in a place there is bright light. Rotate them every two weeks so each plant gets a periodic vacation in the sun.

No place in your home gets bright sun for plants

• Choose plants with wide leaves. These are most likely to have grown on the forest floor and can tolerate low light. They include philodendron, calathea, and spathiphyllum.

• Or add a spot grow light to the area to build up the light.

Houseplants are fuller on one side

• Turn each plant a quarter turn every week so each part of it will get the same amount of light and it will grow evenly all around. Make sure to always turn the plant in the same direction. (I turn my plants clockwise.)

Houseplants are root-bound

• Take the plant out of the pot and cut 2–5" off the root ball. Add fresh potting soil in the bottom of the pot and put the plant back in the same pot. The plant will grow new roots in the fresh soil.

Plants are too tall

• Most houseplants can be cut back without any problem. Be sure you're using a good pruner, and cut just above a leaf. To shape the plant, prune where you see a leaf pointed in the direction you want a new shoot to grow.

Chapter 6
Equipment

CORD, ROPE, AND TWINE

Don't You Hate It When...

There's no place to store cords, ropes, and twine

• For outdoor extension cords, use a hose reel.

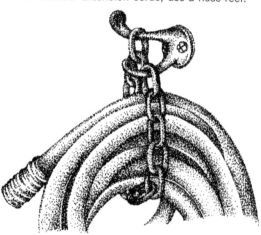

• For bulky cords and ropes, mount a double coat hook (with one hook located slightly below the other). Hang one end of a short piece of chain from the lower hook, loop the chain around the coiled cord or rope, and then attach the other end of the chain to the upper hook.

• To dispense thin twine, nail a metal funnel to a garage wall. Drop a ball of twine inside and thread the twine through the stem. Hang an old pair of scissors next to the funnel.

Garden twine isn't stretchy enough

• Cotton T-shirts cut into strips are strong but also have some "give." Lay the shirt on a hard, flat surface and cut it in 1" strips, working from the bottom up.

• Or make a super-sized rubber band by cutting off the elastic waistband from pantyhose.

You don't like the look of garden twine tied around your plants

• Long, narrow Siberian iris leaves, cut into strips, are sturdy and make great-looking "twine" to secure plants to a stake.

• Morning glory or any tough vine makes great "twine" too.

FENCING AND PATHWAYS

Attractive fencing is costly

• Make garden barriers with red dogwood branches. Bend each branch into a hoop and stick both ends into the soil. That's the start of a cute little fence.

Pathway pavers are really expensive

• Broken pieces of concrete sidewalk make excellent pavers for a garden path. Place the smooth side down; the other side, usually studded with pebbles, looks better. Then plant between the pieces, and the concrete steps will blend right into the natural surroundings.

HOSES AND HOSE GUIDES

Soaker hoses won't stay in place

• Use wire coat hangers to make large staples. Cut off the top, then cut the bottom of the hanger in half, and bend it as needed. The same "staple" can be used to secure row covers and garden cloches (plant covers).

Hoses don't last very long

• A good quality hose will last longer. Look for a hose that feels heavy for its size and resists when you squeeze it hard; that has multiple plies (at least five or six); and that is double-stranded, with mesh that's closely spaced. Rubber is stronger and longer lasting than vinyl, but some vinyl in the composition will make the hose lighter and more kink-resistant.

• Keep a drained hose indoors in cold climates.

• In a hot climate, keep an outdoor hose full of water so it won't bake. (But let the water run awhile before you turn the hose on the plants, since heated water can harm them.)

• Almost all hoses eventually kink up because of repeated heating and cooling. Though most good hoses come with lifetime warranties, most consumers don't bother to take advantage of them.

The garden hose looks untidy when it's all sprawled out

• Keep it neat, tidy, and coiled in a round laundry basket. If you don't like its color, coat it with spray paint that's formulated for plastic.

• Or coil hose as in Fig. A or Fig. B.

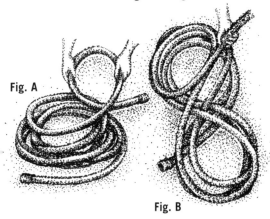

Fig. A

Fig. B

You don't know how to coil a hose for winter

• Turn a large, round trash can upside down and coil the hose around it. Tie the ends together to prevent the hose from unwinding. When the hose is completely wrapped, turn the trash can over and lift it out of the coil. Tie the hose together with Velcro® strips and store it for the winter.

Mike's Pick:
Longest-Lasting Hose Reel

• Flimsy reels with plastic connections are hard to use and fall apart easily. Not Rapid Hose Reel™. Made of heavy-duty steel with solid brass fittings, it's rated at 150 PSI (pounds per square inch) and has a life expectancy of over 10 years. They're expensive but worth every cent.

Hose guides are either too flimsy or expensive

• Without a guide, a hose gets caught, runs over flowers, and knocks pots over. (It's a regular horror movie: *Hoses Gone Wild*.) Since attractive commercial ones are expensive, make your own.

Fig. A   **Fig. B**

• Use copper piping to make a strong hose
guide. You'll need two pieces of ridged copper
piping, one 24" long and 1" in diameter (A), the
other 12" long and 2" in diameter (B). Ask your
local hardware store to cut the pipe and sand
off the copper burrs at the ends of the pipe.
You'll also need a copper pipe cap 1" in diameter
and a galvanized washer 3" in diameter (C)
with a 1½" hole (D). Put the cap on top of A,
and use a mallet to pound A into a flat piece of
ground until only half remains above the surface.
Slip the washer over A so the washer is lying
flat on the ground. Then slip B over A. When
the hose passes it, B will spin around A so there
will be no friction against the hose even if the
hose goes around a corner. You can screw a
decorative finial (E) on top.

• Or make one with two terra-cotta pots. Set them on top of one another, open end to open end, and push a dowel through the drainage holes to anchor them into the ground. Position a set at each corner of the garden bed.

• Or use two black plastic nursery pots, drilling holes into them. Though less attractive than terra cotta, they're more durable.

• Or convert decorative wooden drapery pole finials into hose guides.

MARKERS

You can't remember what's growing where

• Make plant markers with spring-type clothespins and a marking pen. Write the identifying information on the clothespin and clip it to the sides of a seed-starting tray or a pot.

• Plastic flatware also makes good plant markers. Identify the plant by writing on the handle with a marking pen.

• Or cut mini-blinds into 6" pieces.

• Use a permanent marker to label both ends of any homemade marker. If one side fades, the side that is in the ground will not so it will still be legible. (Now let's hope you can remember where your glasses are.)

Plant markers don't blend into the garden

• Flat rocks can become attractive markers. Using acrylic paint and a small artist's brush, paint the name of the plant on one side and any other information on the other. Weatherproof the rock with a coat of clear acrylic, and simply place it in front of the plant for easy identification. This looks especially great in an herb garden.

• Birch-bark tags give a natural look to a garden. Use cut-down, not live ones, and if the bark isn't fresh, soak it in water overnight. With a utility knife, score a rectangle in the bark and pull away several outer layers of birch with a pair of pliers. Write the name of the plant in permanent marker. Use a hole-puncher to make a hole in the bark, thread a piece of twine through the hole, and tie the birch marker to trees, shrubs, or plant stakes.

PERSONAL EQUIPMENT

You can't hear what's happening in the house when you're working in the garden

• Use a baby monitor.

• Of course this may be the reason you're in the garden in the first place.

There's no outdoor sink for hand washing

• Put a bar of soap into a leg of ripped panty-hose and tie it to the outdoors faucet. Scrubbing up will be much more satisfactory.

Garden hands won't come clean

• Unlined driving gloves make wonderful gardening gloves.

• For added protection when doing a dirty job, cover each of your fingers with adhesive sports tape before putting on gloves. The tape comes off easily and leaves no sticky residue behind.

• Coat hands with hand lotion and scrape your fingernails over a bar of soap before putting on gloves.

• You can clean the dirtiest hands by wetting a denture tablet and rubbing your nails with it. Make sure you get some of the lather under your nails, then wash with soap and water.

• Use your old electric toothbrush to remove stubborn garden dirt from under your fingernails. (If it didn't save your gums, at least maybe it can keep your nails clean.)

The knees of your favorite gardening jeans are shot

• Lay them on the table and apply a puddle of clear silicone caulk to each knee. Spread the caulk around with a plastic knife or putty knife until you've covered the whole knee area. Let it dry.

Your shoes get covered with mud

• Spray WD-40® on your boots before working in a muddy yard. The mud will rinse off easily.

Dirt gets tracked indoors when you're doing yard work

• You won't have to remove your shoes or worry about bringing in dirt if you place oversized slip-ons at the door. Slide your shoes right inside them just before you go inside.

• Or leave a couple of shower caps at the door and slip them over your shoes before going inside.

Your arms get beaten up when cutting down shrubs

• Make arm gaiters with a worn pair of crew socks. Cut off the toes, and slip one on each arm from the wrist to the elbow. They'll protect your arms and they aren't too hot to wear in the summer sun.

Your garden gloves aren't organized

• If you have garden gloves piled in a heap in the garden shed, get them organized. Nail several clothespins to the front face of a shelf in the garage or the shed, and then clip a pair of gloves to each. Bonus: They'll be dry when you wear them again.

You can't find a pair of garden gloves that fit

• Try golf gloves, which are usually perfectly sized. But remember that golf gloves are sold individually (for right or left hand), so be sure to purchase one of each. Pick them up on sale at the end of the golf season.

POTS

Terra-cotta pots look too new

• Turn a new pot into a moss-covered treasure. Pour half a cup of buttermilk into a blender. Add enough potter's red or white clay (from a ceramic supply store) until the mixture is the consistency of light gravy, and blend. Add a few tablespoons of moss, and blend for a few seconds more. Spread a thin layer of the mixture on the pot and let it dry. Fill the pot with potting soil, then water the soil and set the pot in the shade. Keep the soil moist and occasionally mist the pot exterior lightly with water. You'll see moss growth in three to four weeks, and within a season the pot will look really aged. Caution: Too much fertilizer can kill moss. Paint the inside of the pot with marine varnish so the fertilizer won't seep through; or put your plant in a plastic pot, and place the plastic pot inside the terra cotta one.

• Also, milk-based glue, such as white school glue, seems to encourage moss growth on pots. Combine 2 tablespoons of white glue with a few tablespoons of ground moss in 1 quart of water. Brush the mixture on the pot. When the pot dries, go ahead and plant in it. Be sure to spray the pot occasionally with a mist of water.

• To speed up moss growth, glue a pot on which moss is already growing on top of a new, upside-down clay pot. Moisten both pots, and the spores from the moss-covered pot on top will quickly spread to the bottom one.

Garden walkways or walls look too new

• Grow moss by blending a few tablespoons of live moss with a cup of buttermilk and pouring it in between stones.

• Use the same method to age a new brick walkway, but take care: It may become slippery.

Plants in terra-cotta pots dry out too quickly

• Hydrate a clay pot by soaking it in water overnight before you put a new plant in it.

• Paint the inside of the clay pot with marine varnish to prevent it from wicking up water. (Bonus: The varnish will also keep white deposits from forming.)

• Or place a plastic pot inside a terra-cotta pot.

Terra-cotta pots stick together and crack

• Put a similar sized peat pot between small terra-cotta pots before you stack and store them. They'll come apart easily.

• Layer newspaper between larger pots.

Terra-cotta pots crack

• Glue the pieces of a pot that has cracked together, and keep them together by wrapping about 15 turns of twine or copper wire around the pot below the rim. It looks great and will keep the pot secure. (Don't you wish there were such an easy way to deal with human crackpots?)

There are many dirty pots and no sink to wash them in

• Fill a wheelbarrow with a 1:9 mixture of bleach and warm sudsy water, and let the pots soak for a while. They're much easier to scrub after a soak. Put them on a hard surface (not on grass), rinse them with a hose, and let them air dry.

You don't have good drainage for your potted plants

• The grates from a discarded gas stove are ideal as "feet." Ask the folks at your local recycling center to save them for you. (Don't tell them why. Maybe they'll have fun speculating.)

PUMP SPRAYS

Pump spray clogs all the time

• The clogs are chemical residue that sticks to the fine-screen filters in the pump or spray hose and inside the little nozzle. Take the sprayer apart. With a toothbrush and an all-purpose cleaner, clean all the screens. Soak the sprayers in a cup of water with a few tablespoons of vinegar to remove mineral deposits that may also be clinging to it.

SPRINKLERS

An inexpensive water sprinkler keeps tipping over

• To make a budget-priced water sprinkler stay put, pull the hose through a cinderblock brick with holes, and then attach the hose to the sprinkler. Now it won't travel while it's in use.

A sprinkler doesn't water far enough

• Place the sprinkler on an old bar stool and it'll water a larger area. Secure it to the stool with bar locks from the hardware store, and make sure the stool won't tip over once the sprinkler is on. (Don't you think this is a nice way for a bar stool to end its days?)

STAKES

Plant stakes cost a bundle

• Use a plastic coffee can lid and four slender bamboo stakes. With a utility knife, cut a large hole in the middle of the lid for the plant to grow through, then make four X cuts near the edge of the lid. Push the stakes through the X's, then make sure the cuts are small enough so you can slide the lid up as the plant grows.

• Or use copper piping and heavy-gauge wire to make a very sturdy stake. You need a 30" length of copper pipe. On both sides of the pipe, 1" from the top, drill holes large enough to accept a piece of 10-gauge black, plastic-coated wire. Thread a 3' piece of wire through one hole, then bend it halfway back around the pipe; repeat on other side. Make 1" hooks on both ends of the wire with pliers. The hooked ends can be connected to make a large support or can be left open to support a few stems. (You can adjust the wire and pipe length for your needs.)

You don't have a tall enough stake

• Willow stems and sunflower stalks (from last summer) make great stakes.

• Or recycle an old pool cue, a fishing rod, a broken golf club, or curtain rods as stakes.

TOOLS

Your tools are too big to work with small plants and seedlings

• For a trowel, use a shoehorn.

• Or use a metal ice cream scoop. It makes the perfect hole into which to transplant smaller nursery plants.

• Use a plastic grapefruit knife or a cocktail fork to transplant seedlings.

There's no place to hang the tools in your shed or garage

• Recycle a rake with a broken handle. Turn the rake portion upside down and nail it to a wall, tines facing outward.

No tool caddy suits all situations

• Some don't wheel well, others have to be lugged around, and most can't carry long-handled tools. The best solution is an old golf bag that has a good set of wheels attached. Pack the bag with fertilizer and garden gloves. Hang trowels and other small tools from the bag.

• If your concern is hand tools only, wear a carpenter's apron. The two large pockets are perfect for carrying pruning tools, a knife, a trowel, a pair of scissors, twine, and more.

You can't find your hand tools

• In the jungle of your garden, hand tools can get lost. To easily locate lost tools, spray-paint the handles with phosphorescent paint.

• If others tend to borrow the tools, paint them in a distinctive color and they'll be easily rec-ognizable as yours.

• The guys in the family won't walk off with your tools if you paint the handles pink.

It's time to clean tools

• Keep tools clean throughout the season and they'll last a lifetime. In your garden shed or garage, fill a 5-gallon bucket with coarse sand, and stir in 1 pint of linseed oil. To clean a tool when you've finished using it, knock the soil off it, plunge it into the bucket, and towel it off. Wipe a little linseed oil on the wood handles too. You'll clean and oil the tool at the same time.

• Or coat tools after use with a light coating of WD-40® or Armor All®.

• If dirt is stuck to a tool, a hard-bristled brush or an old barbecue brush will loosen it.

Tree sap clogs the teeth of a pruning saw

• The sticky residue will come off with oven cleaner. Spray it on, let set for a few minutes, then brush with an old toothbrush. Rinse, dry, and lubricate with a little oil or WD-40®.

Mike's Pick:
Highest-Quality Pruner

• Swiss-made Felco® has forged aluminum handles and hardened steel blades that stay sharp for a very long time. If ever a blade does need replacing, you can pop it off easily and insert a new one. There are right- and left-handed models, and the pruner has a lifetime guarantee.

WHEELBARROWS AND CARTS

Your wheelbarrow tub is rusted and worn thin

• A sheet metal shop may be able to patch it.

Wheelbarrow handles cut into your hands

• For a cushioned grip, use foam pipe insulation. Just cut it to fit and tape it on with duct tape.

• Or fold a mouse pad around each handle, and wrap it with duct tape. (Use high-quality tape. The cheap stuff frays and becomes sticky after use.)

Garden carts lose their wheels

• Some tricycle tires are a perfect fit.

WATERING CAN

A watering can is too heavy

• A gallon of water weighs 8 pounds so keep that in mind when purchasing a water can. A can that is too big will be too heavy to lift and carry when full.

Mike's Pick:
Best Watering Can

• Haws watering can with a long-reach spout is easy to carry and can be tipped with one hand. Perfect if you do a lot of hand watering and want to water with both hands: you can use two cans the same size to keep balanced as you walk. It waters seedlings gently too. Make sure you mark your can so you'll be able to identify it, just in case some-body borrows it. (You'll never get it back if you don't.)

Your watering can rusts

• In between uses, turn the can upside down so it can drain and dry completely.

**Chapter 7
Chores**

COMPOSTING

Don't You Hate It When...

You don't know the right proportions for your compost pile

• Use one part green material (such as grass clippings, alfalfa mulch, cut stems, vegetable scraps, and/or kelp extract) to two parts brown material (such as leaves, straw, dried perennial stems, peat moss, and sawdust). Make alternating layers, each a few inches thick, in a container. Dampen each layer with a hose as you lay it down.

• For more information on composting, a great book is *Let It Rot* by Stu Campbell (Storey Communications).

The compost pile doesn't heat up

• Your brown material isn't coarse enough, the pile is less than a cubic yard in size, or everything isn't moist enough.

• The easiest way to aerate the compost pile is by using a cordless drill with a bulb-planter attachment that can reach the bottom.

The compost pile smells

• You've used too much green material, it's too wet, or it's clumping. Add more brown material. Make sure the pile is covered with a tarp.

There's no brown material for compost in the summer

• Use sawdust and wood ashes for brown material in the summer. But be sure to get real hardwood ash, not ash from pressed logs or treated lumber. (Don't use charcoal or charcoal ashes, either).

There's no green material for compost in the fall

• Kelp extract, available all year long at your garden center, will keep the compost pile cooking. Lay a 3" layer of chopped leaves in the compost. Combine ½ cup of kelp extract with a gallon of water. Sprinkle ½ gallon per 16 square feet (4'x4') of surface. Add another 3" layer of chopped leaves and another ½ gallon of the mixture. This "green" liquid will help break down leaves easily.

You get sticker shock from a composter

• Use a large plastic trash can with a clip-on lid instead. Just drill about a hundred holes, about ½" in diameter and 4" apart, in the sides. Follow the usual composting technique of layering brown and green materials. When the can is full, secure the lid, tip it on its side and roll it around. You'll have compost in a month or so.

• Make a compost bin out of 10 straw bales: Stack the bales on top of each other to form a U-shape. When the bales start to decompose in a couple of years, toss them into a new compost pile.

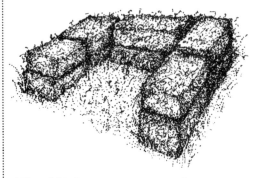

The kitchen scraps you're saving for compost are offensive to the household

• In the winter, collect your vegetable peelings, tea bags, coffee grounds, and eggshells in a garage can, placed in a convenient outdoor spot. Dump the accumulation, together with straw mulch, into the compost, in spring.

• Or bury the frozen kitchen scraps in the garden. Mark the spot so you can dig up the "black gold" in two months.

• Or accumulate the scraps in grocery plastic bags and store them in the freezer until you can add them to the composter.

• Or put everyone on notice that when their parts of the house are in perfect condition, you'll deal with the aroma of the compost heap.

EDGING, PRUNING, AND TRIMMING

The border is not perfectly edged

• Instead of a spade, use a sharp carving knife and a 2x4 piece of lumber at least 8' long as a guide. If you need a guide for curved edges, get a strip of flexible plastic molding at a building supply or hardware store and hold it in place with rocks, brick, or large fabric staples.

Trimming shrubs and trees makes a mess

• Before you begin to work, place a flat plastic sled underneath the area. Catch the cut branches in the sled and pull it to the compost or chipping area.

• Put a large plastic tarp around the trunks to cut down on cleanup time.

Ornamental grasses have to be cleared

• In the fall, wrap bungee cords around clumps of ornamental grasses. Cut them down with an electric hedge clipper and use the bundles as fall decorations around the yard.

FERTILIZING AND WATERING

You don't know whether to use granular or liquid fertilizer

• Always alternate the two types. Liquids can be absorbed through the foliage as well as the root and so they feed plants quickly, but they can also wash away quickly. Granular fertilizers give a steady flow of nutrients. A combination gives the plant quick energy and a steady diet.

Mike's Pick:
The Best 100% Natural Fertilizer

• One application of Alfalfa And More™ will fertilize your plants all season long. Unlike chemical fertilizers it doesn't deplete the soil of its organic matter and microbial activity which causes the soil to become compact and lifeless. The combination of ingredients is super. To buy each ingredient separately would cost a bundle.

You don't understand the numbers on a fertilizer bag

• Every package has three numbers. The first indicates the percentage of nitrogen, the second, the percentage of phosphorous, and the third, the percentage of potassium. So a fertilizer marked l0-54-10 is 10% nitrogen (which promotes green growth); 54% phosphorous (which aids in the growth of flowers and fruit); and 10% potassium (which develops strong stems and roots). Lawn fertilizer generally has a high first number; fertilizer for flowering plants generally has a high middle number.

Fertilizer is difficult to apply

• Fill a disposable aluminum bread pan with bone meal or granular fertilizer. Squeeze the sides of the pan and pour the bone meal into holes with newly planted bulbs, or apply the fertilizer around the base of large plants.

Mike's Pick:
The Best Liquid Fertilizer

• Drammatic® Liquid Plant Fish Food processes a whole fish into a liquid concentrate. It contains all the essential minerals, unlike many of the other fish products. Visit their website at www.fishfertilizer.com.

Fertilizer causes your plants to "burn"

• One of the biggest mistakes gardeners make is to apply too much fertilizer. It's so important to follow the label directions perfectly. I added too much fertilizer to my hydrangea plants one summer and the stems got long and weak. They were drooping even before the flowers bloomed.

Your garden isn't as green as you would like

• When plant leaves are yellow or pale, it's a sign they need more magnesium, an essential part of chlorophyll, which makes plants green. (Plants need magnesium to use nitrogen, phosphorous, and sulfur and produce flowers and fruit.) Epsom salts, which contain magnesium, are the solution.

• In your perennial bed, once a year only, in spring, rake 1 cup of Epsom salts into about every 25 square feet of surface soil along with your regular fertilizer.

• For roses and tomatoes, starting in spring, sprinkle 1 teaspoon of Epsom salt per 1' of plant height around their bases. Repeat every 4 to 6 weeks throughout the summer.

• For healthy foliage for all plants, add 4 teaspoons of Epsom salts to 1 gallon of water, and spray leaves twice a month or monthly. Do not spray when plants need watering or when temperatures are above 80° F.

You have to bend when fertilizing trees and shrubs

• Get a plastic bird-feeder filler that has an opening that slides and a piece of PVC that's wide enough for the bird-feeder filler to fit snugly inside it. Put granular fertilizer into the filler, insert the filler into the pipe and open the filler to release the fertilizer at the plant's drip-line (where water falls when it rains).

Daily watering becomes a nuisance

• A weekly soaking is better than daily watering. An inch a week is ideal for most plants.

• For best results use soaker hoses. They'll water the roots where needed, and they conserve water, too.

You left the hose on too long

• While newly planted trees and shrubs need slow, long soaking, you don't want to overdo it. Be sure to set the kitchen timer to remind you when it's time to turn off the hose or turn it onto another garden spot.

LIFTING AND MOVING

A big rock can't be budged

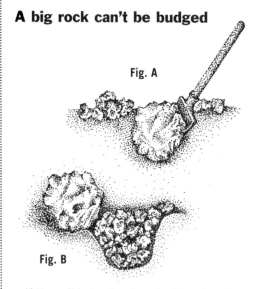

Fig. A

Fig. B

• If the soil is hard, soften it with water, then remove as much as possible from all around the rock. Next, wedge your shovel or pry bar under the rock, lean your weight on the handle to pry up the rock a bit, then put a stone between the rock and the ground (Fig. A). Repeat the process until you've wedged enough stones under the rock to bring it to ground level, then roll it where you want it (Fig. B).

A big rock or a big bag of fertilizer is too heavy to move

• Lay a wheelbarrow on its side, with the edge pushed up against the object you want to lift. Then, slowly push the object inside the wheelbarrow. Go to the other side. Using both hands, keeping your knees bent, and standing as closely as possible to the wheelbarrow, grab the undercarriage and pull the wheelbarrow upright. Take care not to strain your back.

A shrub or small tree is too heavy to move

• Lay it on a large round snow sled.

• Or put it on a large snow shovel that you can pull like a sled.

MULCHING

You can't figure out which mulch to use

• One-season mulches such as chopped alfalfa, finely ground fir bark, cocoa bean shells, and mushroom compost are ideal for annual, perennial or vegetable gardens. They cool the soil, keep moisture in, keep weeds down and in the course of a year, they break down and provide organic matter to the soil.

Mike's Pick:
Best Mulch Mixture

• The mulches mentioned above are all great, but I especially like to mix my own power-packed combination. Not only does it mulch the soil, but also it's loaded with nutrients. On a tarp, combine one 2-cubic-foot bag each of cocoa bean mulch, ground fir bark, and chopped alfalfa mulch. Add two 5-gallon pails of compost and 2 cups of cottonseed meal.

You don't know how thickly to apply the mulch

• For perennials and shallow-rooted shrubs: Spread a 2–3" layer around each plant, but do not pack it around the crowns of plants.

• For shrubs and trees: Spread a 3–4" layer of mulch.

• But there's an exception: Cocoa bean mulch should not be more than 1" thick because it tends to hold water and become moldy. (Caution: Dogs may become gravely ill from chewing on cocoa bean mulch. If you think a dog has eaten any, immediately contact your veterinarian or the ASPCA Animal Poison Control Center at 888-426-4435.)

Stone mulch needs cleaning up

• Use stone mulch around downspouts, since it will catch debris and it won't wash away. Clean it with a leaf vacuum or leaf blower.

• For a big job, there are rock cleaning machines that suck up the rock, clean off the dirt, then return it to its place. Ask a large landscape company if they have this service.

You can't use peat moss

• Peat moss, like oil, is a natural product that can't be renewed. It's so scarce that it's no longer harvested in the British Isles, and while it's still available from Canada, no one knows for how long. Fortunately, there's an ecologically sound substitute—"coconut fiber dust." It's the by-product made from the husks that are left when coconuts are processed for food. Since coconuts are grown on a regular basis, this is a renewable resource. Best of all, coconut fiber dust has texture, is baled, and looks and acts just like peat moss once it is

dried. For more information, check out Coir®
potting soil at www rolanka.com.

You don't know which mulch to choose for winter covering

• In northern climates, nature generally provides a snow covering to protect plants from
cold weather that might kill them. But in years
when snowfalls are light, you may have to give
your perennials some extra help by laying
down a 1' layer of any of the following:

– Fallen oak leaves are a good choice. They
are large but not too big, stay relatively dry,
and don't compact, so they won't smother the
plants that lie underneath them. Avoid maple
leaves and chopped or ground-up leaves. The
former are too big and lay flat in a smothering
blanket; the latter compact quickly and also
smother the perennials. (However, the other
leaves can be put into yard bags. Fill them
halfway, then flatten them into pillows. These
mulch pillows can be used for insulation once
the ground freezes.)

– Straw is a good alternative. It's a great insulator and its hollow stems allow air movement
around the perennials. But if you see a lot of
seed heads in the bale, you'll have problems
in the spring when the wheat, oats, or barley
seed germinate.

– Hay isn't as good an insulator as straw, but it tends to have fewer weed seeds. Canary grass, or marsh hay, is as weed-free a mulch as you can buy and is easy to work in over the garden.

RAKING

Rakes constantly get clogged up with leaves

• Garden centers sell clog-free rakes. They're worth the slight extra cost, and their heavy plastic, pointed teeth are sturdy enough so you can really dig in.

You can't keep the leaf bag open while you're raking

• A 2x3' piece of cardboard placed inside the leaf bag will keep it standing straight. When the bag is half-filled, remove the cardboard. The bag will stand by itself.

• Use a tall bucket instead of your hands to press the leaves into the bag. You'll pack them more tightly and use fewer bags.

Gathering leaves is slow work

• If you're gathering them by hand, use two garbage-can lids as tools.

• Rake leaves onto a plastic tarp, an old bed-spread or sheet, a blanket or a shower curtain, then pull the whole thing to the compost pile.

• Or make a scooper, using a broom handle sawed in half and a big piece of plastic. (You can make one as large as 5x3' from a 100-pound plastic grain bag, or cut open a plastic bag, or use a large old window shade). Roll each of the shorter ends around a piece of broom handle, staple it in place, and you have your tool. Cut a little hole midway down the plastic right next to the piece of broomstick to create a handle that you can slip your fingers through. Lay the scooper on top of the leaf pile and your handle ends together at the bottom to make a tightly packed roll, then carry the leaves to your composter.

Leaves blow all over

• Corral the leaves when they're being blown by using burlap and a few wire rods to set up a V-shaped barrier. Blow the leaves into the V, where they can be easily bagged and not be blown away.

• Turn an old mesh playpen on its side and rake leaves into it. It's the perfect leaf catcher. The leaves can't blow away and when it's full, you can drag the leaves to wherever you want them.

Leaves get caught in the bottom of a shrub

• Use a large shop vac to collect hard-to-remove-leaves.

You have to remove fallen leaves from ground cover

• Even with a blower, this is a long, tedious chore, so prevent the problem by covering the area with bird netting before leaves fall. Come spring or after all the leaves have fallen, lift the netting and leaves off the ground cover.

SOIL PREPARATION

Soil is heavy clay

• Clay soils drain poorly, and most trees (and other plants) won't survive if the root ball sits in a hole filled with water that cannot drain away. To test how quickly the soil will drain, dig a hole as wide as but no deeper than recommended, fill it with water, and then time how quickly the water drains. If the hole is dry after two hours, it's safe to plant the tree; but if there is still water for up to five hours, you need to dig a dry well.

• A dry well is a vertical shaft that lets water move away from the root ball. To dig one, use a posthole digger to go 3–4' straight down or ideally, 3–4' below the root ball hole. Fill the bottom half of the dry well with large round stones and the remainder with smaller rocks. Lay a piece of landscaping fabric over the dry well to help keep soil from filtering into it.

Sod has to be removed for a new bed

• Make your own rich, loamy soil without removing the sod or digging. Place several layers of wet (black-and-white print only) newspaper on the ground. Cover the newspaper with three layers in the following order: grass cuttings, manure, and peat moss, to make a combined layer 2–3" deep. Repeat the previous step until the layers measure at least 10–12" high. In the fall, add a layer of leaves (preferably shredded, because they decompose quickly). If you have soil from potted plants, toss that on top of the leaves. As a final step, cover the layers with wet newspaper and potting soil or mulch. Don't turn or stir the layers. Begin to plant when the layers have the crumbly texture of loamy soil. This layering technique, called "lasagna" soil, is described by Patricia Lanza in *Lasagna Gardening*. But you need patience. The process usually takes at least a year.

SPRAYING

Mike's Pick:
Best Commercial Spray-Pump

- The Gilmour Company makes a great line of sprayers, sized to fit all needs. Available at most garden centers.

You can't remember what chemical was in the spray bottle

- It can be a catastrophe if you spray herbicide on plants you want to protect, and some fungicides can be dangerous on food crops. Even a small amount of residue can do harm. So use three sprayers—one for fungicide, one for insecticide, and one for herbicide. Label them and wash them carefully after use.

You have to mix your own herbicides, fungicides, and insecticides

• An old blender in the garden shed mixes formulas in an instant. Be sure to write "Not for Food Use" on the blender jar. Make sure you clean it thoroughly with soap and water after each use, because you don't want the various chemicals to contaminate one another.

You can't figure out how much pesticide to use

• Instructions for mixing pesticides from concentrates usually call for a tablespoon or a teaspoon per gallon of water. What if you need only a cupful? Since 1 cup (8 ounces) is 1/16 of a gallon (128 ounces), you'll need 1/16 of a teaspoon of pesticide. You calculate that in drops. There are 60 drops in a teaspoon, so 1/16 of a teaspoon is 60 divided by 16, or 3.75 drops—let's say 4.

Plant nutrients and medicines need special handling because they're poisonous

• While thoroughly washing the measuring cups can solve the problem, you'll save time if you make disposable measuring cups with plastic glasses and a permanent marking pen.

Measure two ounces of water into the cup, mark off that measure spot, and then continue to add two ounces at a time, marking the level with each addition.

WEEDING

Mike's Pick:
Best Weeder

• Smith and Hawken® makes the greatest, inexpensive weeder. It comes in both right- and left-handed versions. Check it out at smithandhawken.com.

Weeds grow wild

• Use rhubarb leaves as a weed barrier. After harvesting the tender rhubarb stalks, gather the leaves and place them wherever cover is needed, overlapping them so no surface is exposed. While they will turn yellow, they will serve as a weed barrier into the summer and help keep the soil moist. Later they'll break down and add nutrients to the soil.

• Keep dandelions at bay with an application of corn gluten. It's non-toxic and it destroys the seeds as they try to sprout. For large quantities of corn gluten, shop farm stores.

Digging into soil brings weed seeds to the surface

• To deal with the weeds that sprout in a new bed, prepare the soil by leveling it, breaking it up, and smoothing the surface just as you would to get the garden ready. Tiny weed seeds will begin to sprout. Let them grow until no new seedlings are appearing. Buy a soil prep called "bark fines," which is ground and partly composted fir bark, and sprinkle it over the weed until all the green parts are covered. In a few days, scrape back the fines; if there is still green on the weeds, cover them and wait until weed seedlings have rotted away. Don't dig deeply into the soil or you'll bring up more seeds. Let the bark fines help keep weeds down and soil moist.

• Or clean out a new garden bed easily by spreading plastic or carpet over the area. Seal the edges so all that heat stays under the plastic. Clear plastic acts like a greenhouse, trapping the solar energy. Plants underneath will be "cooked" and the heat will cause all vegetation to decompose. After a few weeks under the plastic, the ground will be plant-free. Remove the plastic, till up the soil, and get that bed ready for planting.

A giant weeding chore faces you

• Don't put off pulling weeds. If you do it daily, it's not so overwhelming.

• Weed after a rainfall or when the garden has been watered (weeds will be easier to pull), but wait until the plants are dry. The wait will allow time for the soil to dry a bit so it won't compact as you walk on it, and it's a little more comfortable weeding around dry plants.

• Weed and hoe in the early morning on a day that's predicted to be hot, sunny and windy. By late afternoon, the hoed weeds will have dehydrated and disappeared. Make sure that the garden is well watered the next morning so the plants you welcome will have a good soak.

• After weeding a flower or perennial garden area, put down a pre-emergent herbicide to prevent new weeds from coming up.

• Weeds with deep root systems, like bindweed, must be killed with a chemical herbicide. If they're pulled by hand, some of the root may remain and the weed will return with a vengeance.

Mike's Pick:
Best Pre-Emergent Herbicide for a Vegetable Garden

• Corn gluten.

Using herbicide on unwanted greenery causes collateral damage

• If you have a weed growing through a hosta or a vine growing through a rose bush, be cautious about how you apply herbicide. Put on a pair of heavy-duty rubber gloves, and slip a pair of absorbent cotton gloves over them. Dip your fingers into the liquid herbicide, and apply it only where it is needed.

• Or dip a clean paintbrush into weed killer and carefully brush the weed.

• Or, when using a powerful weed killer, first cut an inch or two off the bottom of a 2-liter soda bottle and set it over the weed. Place the nozzle of the weed killer into the neck of the bottle and spray. The bottle shields surrounding plants.

• To treat plants in small areas where no other plants will be affected, you don't have to drag out the pump spray to apply pesticide or herbicide. Prepare the solution in a bucket, dip a whiskbroom into the liquid, and carefully shake it over plants.

Weeds are growing in pathways and vegetable rows

• To clear pathways of weeds, put down layers of newspaper in the pathways, and then cover with mulch or chopped leaves.

• Carpet strips make wonderful row cover. Bonus: no matter how much it rains, they will protect your shoes from getting muddy. And if the carpet is made from a natural fiber, it will eventually rot and go back into the soil.

• Weeds in driveways and sidewalks can be killed without collateral damage and without even using herbicides. Just pour white vinegar on them on a warm, sunny day. They'll be gone within 24 hours.

Creeping Charlie takes over

• If Creeping Charlie, an invasive weed, has attacked your lawn, spray it with an herbicide when the purple flowers are about to open. Repeat a week later, and if the weed is still a problem, spray it in the fall after the first white frost on the lawn. The seed will be trying to grow in the spring; use corn gluten to kill it while it is germinating.

There's no place to stash the weeds when you're gardening

• Place large, lightweight attractive garden pots or garden hose containers at strategic places around the gardens. Toss the weeds in as you work. This is a lot more attractive than large garbage pails.

• Fill your pocket with grocery plastic bags. When you run across weeds or twigs, dispose of them in the bag. A bag is also handy if you don't want to touch a weed such as stinging nettle. Just slip the bag over your hand before you pull the weed.

Weed killers aren't effective on vines and trees

• Vine-X® Vine & Brush Control, an herbicide that can be applied to the stems of unwanted plants with a built-in paintbrush, works well on woody vines, small trees, and even thistles. Since it isn't sprayed, it affects only targeted greenery and kills it to the root within a few weeks. Use it in early spring or late into the fall. It's especially good with common or European buckthorn, which grows as a tree, or thicket, chokes out native flora, and drives away native fauna. It's nasty. Check out www.vine-x.com.

Tough little tree seedlings are hard to pull

• Use a pair of pliers. Get a tight grip at the woody base and pull straight up. Works best after a good rain.

Weeds take over

• The presence of weeds is an indication of the quality of your soil. If the soil is more fertile, you'll have fewer weeds overall.

• If you have dandelions, it's a sign your soil lacks calcium.

• Creeping buttercup, chicory, coltsfoot, dandelion, broad-leaved dock and mayweed indicate that your soil is heavy clay.

• Bindweed, golden rod, and sheep sorrel indicate light sandy soil.

• Clover, vetch, rape, and black medick mean your soil needs more nitrogen.

• Sedges, smartweed, hedge nettle, horsetail, and silverweed show that the soil is poorly drained.

• Chamomile, creeping bellflowers, mustard, thistles, and wild carrot indicate alkaline soil.

• Daisies, docks, hawkweed, horsetail, rabbit foot clover, horehound, knotweed, mullein, wild radish, garden sorrel, and wild strawberries indicate acidic soil.

A plant takes over the garden

• Bee balm, bergamot, false dragonhead, lamb's ears, mugwort, obedient plant, mint, wormwood, and yarrow, as well as some asters and many grasses, multiply underground and by summer, they're everywhere. Placing a barrier around the roots helps you contain them. Use a 5-gallon bucket with the bottom cut out; or for a more attractive look, use round or square clay chimney tiles, which look like clay pots without bottoms. Made of fired terra cotta and used to line fireplace chimneys, they're weather-resistant and long lasting. Sink the tile, leaving only 2–3" above ground. Make sure that the plant doesn't send a shoot over the top of the tile and escape into the surrounding soil.

Chapter 8
Diseases, Insects,
and Weather

DISEASE

Don't You Hate It When...

Black spot ruins your rose bush

• Baking soda will clear it up. Mix 1 tablespoon baking soda in 1 gallon of water. Add a few drops of insecticidal soap or liquid dish soap to help the baking soda stick to the plant and soil. Spray the top and bottom of the leaves. Rose bushes that are susceptible to black spot should be sprayed starting in early spring twice a month, once a month if they're resistant to the disease.

"Damping off" fungus attacks seedlings

• The fungus attacks the emerging seedling (usually one that has been started indoors) at the point where the tiny stem meets the soil. The stem rots and the seedling falls over, even though typically it has a healthy green top. Avoid this problem by starting with clean seed boxes and fresh seed starting mix. (Buy seed starter mix, not garden soil.) Moisten the mix, plant and cover the seeds as directed, then sprinkle the surface with finely ground sphagnum moss.

The moss helps reduce the likelihood of damping off by creating an environment that prohibits the growth of the fungus.

• Also put the plants where air circulation is good.

• Once seeds are planted, control damping off with this formula: Add 1 chamomile tea bag to 1 quart of boiling water and leave it for 24 hours. Using a plant mister, spray the seedlings with this chamomile tea each time they are watered.

• Or purchase the commercial product No Damp Off® manufactured by Mosser Lee Company.

Leaves look yellow

• A variety of problems can cause leaves to turn yellow, but if the thin tissue of the leaves turns yellow while the veins are green, the plant may need iron. First test the pH of the soil; if it's not right for your plant, the plant may not be able to draw out the iron. If it is right, add extra iron to the soil. Buy liquid iron in a garden center or make your own. Just drop two pads of fine steel wool into a gallon pail of water. The pads will rust, and in a few weeks, the water will be rich with iron. (Be careful not to get this on driveways, sidewalks, the sides of buildings, or other surfaces that may stain.)

Add a cup of iron water to small plants and gallons to large trees. If the plant still looks yellow by the end of the growing season, give it some more iron water. Iron water keeps for a long time. Just give it a stir before you use it.

Mildew is a problem

• Some of the most beautiful garden plants, including bee balm, delphinium, phlox, lilacs, and roses, attract mildew, a white powdery fungus. The trick is in knowing which plants are susceptible. Providing good air circulation and using fungicides won't cure the problem but may prevent it. A liquid spray of Bonide® Fung-onil will control mildew and other fungus diseases.

• Baking soda will prevent and also fight fungus. To make an effective spray, add 1 tablespoon each of baking soda and horticultural oil (or 1 tablespoon of baking soda and ½ teaspoon of dishwashing soap) to 1 gallon of water. Put the solution in a 1- or 2-gallon hand pump sprayer and shake it thoroughly. Spray the plants in the cool of the morning, continuing to shake the sprayer occasionally as you work. Vulnerable plants should be treated every seven days.

• Another mildew preventive is onion juice. Place a handful of scallions or chives in a

1-gallon glass jar. Fill the jar with water, seal it tightly, place it in a sunny spot (indoors or out) and let the mixture steep for three days. Then strain it through cheesecloth. Spray susceptible plants with this mixture every two weeks as a preventive, or spray infected plants once or twice a week to control infection. The solution will remain effective for a month if it is refrigerated (and not mistaken for salad dressing).

Pines turn a bright orange

• The color is a sign of needle blight, a fungus that affects Austrian and red pine trees. The tree can be sprayed with a fungicide, but large trees or multiple planting can be impossible to treat effectively. Cool, rainy conditions will cause more needles to be infected.

Root rot is affecting plants

• You need to grow new roots. First, dry the soil of a plant afflicted with root rot until it's almost cactus dry. Remove the plant from the pot and cut away 1–2" of old root and soil from the root ball. Wash out the pot with a 1:9 solution of bleach and water. Fill the bottom 1–2" of the pot with fresh potting soil, and replace the plant. Then water the plant with willow water. (See page 68, "Root Cuttings.")

• If the plant remains wilted even after the water treatment, place the plant and pot in a clear plastic bag. Provide strong indirect light and continue to water with willow water when the soil is dry. Continue this treatment until new roots are formed. (See page 68, "Root Cuttings" for willow water.)

Pots spread disease to your plants

• Pots must be disinfected before reuse. Make a 1:9 solution of bleach and water, and use it to scrub inside and outside the container. Rinse it and let it dry before you reuse it.

Spruce trees develop fungal disease

• When spruces are stressed, they can develop Cytospora canker and Rhizosphaera needle-cast. Cytospora causes cankers along the larger branches and trunk that then ooze sap and develop white, crusty areas. It usually starts on the lower limbs that die back and lose their needles. Over the years, as these branches are pruned away, the spruce looks like what I call a Minnesota palm tree. As there is no cure for this disease, the best solution is to plant trees that are resistant to the disease, like "Swiss Stone" Pine. (See page 60.)

Wilt disease makes plants droopy

• Wilt disease is a general term for a lack of water in plant tissue. The two most common forms, verticillium and fusarium, cannot be cured. The most susceptible plants are roses, tomatoes, clematis, and strawberries, but it may affect any annual or perennial and even shrubs and trees. Control it by pruning away the affected plant below the wilted area as soon as possible. Between cuts, clean the pruner with a 1:9 solution of bleach and water so the disease doesn't spread. Remove entirely any plant that dies, and don't replace it with the same type of plant, since the disease can linger in the soil.

INSECTS

You have to use chemicals to control insects

• Try toads for pest control. A toad can eat tons of slugs and insects in a single growing season. Flat stones placed in the shade, then raised off the ground an inch or so, will give them the cool, moist, sheltered place they like. Sink a shallow saucer near the toad house so its rim is just above the surrounding area, and keep it filled with clean, fresh rainwater. If toads don't come on their own, see if you can hire some neighborhood boys to find you some. And don't use chemicals: toads will stay away. (And don't think if you kiss one, it will turn into a prince.)

• Purchase nematodes, tiny worms, to eat pests. From a garden center you can get small, moist sponge squares that hold millions of nematodes. When you fill a watering can with spring or distilled water and put the sponge into the water, they will swim out. Water the problem area with the nematodes, making sure the soil is moist enough for them to move in it. Once the nematode colony is established they will attack the grubs and other soil insects. Bury the sponge in your garden afterward, so that any worms that remain in it can move out into the soil. These garden helpers will remain in the ground for years as long as the area is free of pesticides.

• Garlic has insecticide, antibacterial and antifungal properties. Here's an all-purpose homemade insect spray, which will fight disease, too: Boil a quart of water with two crushed garlic bulbs (skin and all), one small finely chopped onion and 1 tablespoon cayenne pepper. Let set overnight, then add 1 tablespoon of liquid dish soap before straining through cheesecloth and transferring the mixture to a sprayer. To store, cover tightly and use within two weeks.

• Plant cloves of garlic around rose bushes and most insects will stay clear. Don't harvest these garlic plants, though.

• Because they are poisonous, rhubarb leaves are rarely eaten by bugs and animals. Fill a large jar with chopped rhubarb leaves, pour hot water over all, and seal the jar. Place it in a sunny spot for three or four days, strain the liquid and place it in a spray bottle to use as an all-purpose bug spray. The tea will be potent for about a week.

• One of the safer products to kill indoor and outdoor crawling insects contains diatomaceous earth, a mineral product that is ground into a powder. Though it doesn't harm humans, when cockroaches, ants, fleas, silverfish, and other insects crawl through it, the sharp edges of the powder cut them so that they dehydrate and die.

• Borage, a self-sufficient herb, self-sows and grows where it's happy, in a sunny place in dry soil. Its attractive blue flowers look great in a salad. Since it absorbs minerals, it's an excellent addition to the fall compost pile. Also, it attracts bees and repels Japanese beetles in the strawberry bed and hornworms in the tomato garden.

8 Diseases, Insects, and Weather

8 Diseases, Insects, and Weather

• Try mint insecticide on everything from aphids to cabbage moths. Bring 2 quarts of water to a boil, remove the water from the heat, and place a 100% green tea bag in it. Then add 1 cup of finely chopped mint to the cooling liquid and let it steep overnight. In the morning strain the liquid through a piece of cheesecloth. In the evening, spray a sample of the liquid on a test plant or branch. Check in the morning, and if there is no negative change in the appearance of the plant, the liquid is ready to go; but if the plant doesn't look well, add some fresh water to your insecticide tea. (Mints from different gardens are chemically different, and plants react to them differently as well. So it's important to do a test before spraying the whole garden.)

Mike's Pick:
Best Commercial Insect-Spray

• Just look for any product that contains neem oil. Not only does it kill insects, but also it prevents fungus diseases, and it can be used on most plants including edible ones. It's virtually harmless to most beneficial insects and is also safe around kids and pets. Neem oil products are available at most garden centers.

You need a quick remedy for any kind of insect

• When you don't have the time or ingredients for the preceding remedies, use commercially prepared onion juice. Add 1 tablespoon and a few drops of insecticidal soap to 1 quart of water and spray any vegetable or garden plant.

• To get rid of an infestation fast, use a shop vac filled with 1" of water and a squirt of liquid dish soap to suck up bugs in the garden, patio, or sidewalk. The soap in the water will ensure that they don't escape.

Vegetable crops are being attacked

• To help cauliflower, onions, beets, and turnips resist insects and disease, sprinkle hardwood ash at the base of the plants.

• To protect cabbage from bugs, nothing works better than cayenne pepper. Mix 2 tablespoons of cayenne and 8 drops of dish soap in 1 gallon of water. Let sit overnight, stir, and strain thoroughly before spraying on the cabbage each week.

Ants are bothering you

• Mix 4 tablespoons of maple or corn syrup and 1 teaspoon of borax. Put a dab of this mixture into small, lidded plastic containers and then poke a few holes in the lids large enough for the ants to enter. Set the covered containers in areas frequented by ants.

• Or mix equal amounts of powdered sugar and borax and place in containers.

• You don't need chemicals to get rid of ants, even fire ants, in the garden or lawn. Remove the top and bottom lids from a 5-pound coffee can and put the cylinder over the nest in the early evening when ants have returned home. Push the can into the ground to make a seal around the nest. Boil a large quantity of water and take the teakettle or pot to the anthill and pour as much as you can into the can. This should kill the whole colony.

You've got ants on your plants

• Ants climbing your plant stems are looking for natural plant nectar (like the drops you see on peonies) or honeydew, a sweetish deposit secreted by aphids and scale insects. Look closely, and if you observe aphids or scale, spray the plant with insecticidal soap. However, ants may reintroduce aphids and scale when they come around to harvest the honeydew. Prevent their returning to a sprayed plant by smearing petroleum jelly around the base of the main stem to create a barrier. Make sure no part of the plant touches another.

Aphids, blackflies, and whiteflies are on your plants and soil

• Yellow sticky traps (available in garden centers in various sizes) attract these critters.

• Or make your own with yellow electrician's tape from the hardware store. Wrap an ice cream stick, a wooden plant label, or even an old pencil with the tape (sticky side out) overlapping it to make a solid yellow surface. Place stakes wherever there is a problem and watch the tiny insects land on the attractive yellow surface and be trapped. When the stake is full of insects, dispose of it and put in a new one.

Apple maggots are spoiling your crops

• Stop apple fruit flies from laying eggs. At after-Christmas clearance sales, buy red plastic Christmas tree balls. Coat them with spray adhesive in spring and hang three to six in each tree, more in larger trees. The flies are attracted to red and will get stuck in the adhesive. Once balls are covered with flies, replace them with new ones.

• Or lure them to a soda bottle trap. Stir a tablespoon of molasses into 1 cup of water. Pour the mixture into the bottle and lay it on its side. Flies will come in and can't get out. While organic controls aren't 100% effective, these two traps together work very effectively.

Ash plant bug is destroying the leaves of green and white ash

• Ash plant bug eggs, left in crevices in the bark, hatch in early spring. By the time the striping and mottling on the leaf surface are visible in summer, the time for effective control is past. Stop the insect in spring in the nymph stage, just after eggs hatch, when the first buds and leaves appear. Spray the tree with Malathion (according to the instructions on the label) and repeat seven to ten days later. This should reduce the bug population and minimize damage.

A bee, hornet, or wasp stings you

• Immediately apply non-flavored meat tenderizer and a dab of water to make a paste. Meat tenderizer contains papain, an enzyme derived from papaya that stops itching and pain. Make sure the stinger is removed too.

• Any of the following can relieve the pain of a bee sting: leaves of weed plantain, the leaves or stems of mint, the leaves of bee balm, or the flowers of calendula. Familiarize yourself with how they look, or mark them so you will be ready in the event of a bee sting. Crush the leaf, stem, or flower, and rub the stung area with the sap. Repeat until the pain is reduced.

Birch leaf miner is attacking paper birch

• Most gardeners don't notice the problem until the damage is severe. By then the larvae may have dropped off the leaf and formed a pupa (the state in an insect's life when it forms a sheath around itself) in the ground. Once you have this problem, it will recur. Spray the birch tree with a systemic insecticide when the lilacs are at their peak of bloom and spray again twice, a week apart. If you can break the cycle in the spring, you'll reduce the size of the next generation, so it will cause less damage.

Box elder bugs are taking over

• They're not harmful to people or plants but if their presence (on a southern or western wall) is bothering you, remove them with a jet of soapy water. They feed off box elder trees; if you get rid of the box elder trees, you'll get rid of box elder bugs. (You can't say the same of bedbugs.)

Cane borers attack your roses

• When you notice larvae of insects burrowing down the center of a rose cane, pesticides can't be guaranteed to control them. The best cure: use a bit of white glue to seal the tip of each cane after you prune it. When it is dry, the glue is impenetrable to invaders. Use a systemic insect spray, too.

Gnats are on the attack

• Try a bug repellent and a wide-brimmed straw hat. Spray only the underside of the brim, not your skin. Gnats don't like to fly underneath—and the repellent should shoo them off anyway.

Japanese beetles take over roses

• Japanese beetles love rose leaves and flowers, so the roses will be the first plants they attack. But don't let that deter you from planting roses. In fact, the roses keep the beetles contained to one area. Pick them off and discard them in a can of soapy water.

Slugs are a problem

• Sprinkle caffeinated coffee grounds around slug-loving plants. The grounds kill the slugs and are also good for the soil.

• Or make green cabbage leaves into loose rolls, then secure them with toothpicks or rubber bands. Make enough to place them in the infected garden about 3' apart. Soak them in water, drain off the excess liquid, and put them down in the early evening on a warm night. Pick them up in the morning and toss them in a bucket of very warm water, and you'll see dead slugs. Put them back down the next night, near to but not exactly in the same spots as on the previous evening. Repeat the process until the infestation subsides, reusing the rolls or making new ones.

• See "You have to use chemicals to control insects" at the beginning of this chapter.

Mike's Pick:
Best Commercial Slug Remedy

• Sluggo®, made from iron phosphate, is safe around kids, pets, and birds. Use it in the spring before damage is evident. Applied a few times a year, it eliminates slugs for many years. Available at most garden centers or visit sluggo.com.

Scale, whitefly, and mealy bug are hard to get rid of

• Bonide® All-Season Spray Oil works on these bugs by smothering them. Spray the plant thoroughly. Use this product indoors and out any time of the year. Note: Be careful when using oily sprays in the house. They attract dirt and dust and may stain your carpet.

Spider mites have attacked

• Bonide® Mite X which is non-poisonous and contains clove oil, is great indoors and out to help plants infested with spider mites.

Wasps are spoiling your fun

• Buy a wasp trap from the garden centers. . All of them work by luring the insect into the trap where it dies, because it can't get out.

• Or make a trap with an uncapped soda bottle on its side with an an inch of fresh (still carbonated) cola in the bottom. Place it away from humans. Tie a piece of foil around the neck of the bottle and bring one end down about one inch away from the opening. The insect will be lured inside, then try to escape, but he'll fly toward the light that shines through the bottle rather than toward the dark (the opening, obscured by the foil), so he's trapped.

• Or repel wasps with the aroma of lemon grass, lemon verbena, or lemon balm. Harvest them just before the outdoor event starts, crush them to release their oils, and place them under a low basket turned upside down. (You can even put a decorative flower arrangement on the basket to decorate the table.) The oils will work their magic through the loose weave of the basket.

• Of course, wasps are beneficial insects because they eat the bad guys. If they aren't bothering you or you're not using the yard, don't leave the traps out.

Wasps are spoiling your fun

• For some crazy reason hornets love the smell of vinegar. Add a few inches of white vinegar to a few plastic water or soda bottles and set them around the infested area. You can even take along a bottle or two to an outdoor restaurant to keep hornets away while you dine.

WEATHER PROBLEMS

Flowers and shrubs start budding too early

• A late-winter hot spell followed by a cold snap may damage the leaf but it won't prevent them from surviving. Even if the primary leaf is killed, secondary buds will usually leaf out.

Spring frost kills early plantings

• If low temperatures threaten, cover baby plants with cardboard boxes (which come in all sizes and can be collapsed and stored when not in use). Make sure to remove them when the weather turns sunny and warmer.

• Or cover the young plants with coffee cans or pillowcases.

• A 24" oscillating fan will move enough air to prevent frost damage on a 10x20' garden. If the garden is longer than 20', you'll need a fan for every 10' of width. Place the fan so it blows over your garden, not directly on the plants, so don't set it on the ground.

The garden looks droopy and stressed on hot summer days

• Plant Russian sage, which comes in many strains and whose cool blue blooms withstand the heat and bloom from July through September. It needs full sun and non-irrigated, well-drained soil. The tall stately spikes of delicate purple/blue flowers aren't as showy as individual flowers, but as a whole, the plant can really make a show in the garden.

Fall frost kills the impatiens

• Keep them blooming—indoors. Dig up two or three of the smaller plants and move them into decorative pots. As winter houseplants, they like a sunny spot and moist soil.

Winter kills plants with soft crowns

• The soft crowns of delphinium, hollyhock, garden mum, foxglove, carnations, and Canterbury bells are easily smothered under wet winter cover, especially if the ground hasn't frozen first. Once the ground has frozen and before laying down mulch, give these plants additional protection. You'll need a nursery pot large enough to accommodate the crown of the plant. Fill the pot loosely with dried leaves, and cut down the plant enough so that the pot can be turned upside down over it. Press down on the pot so rodents can't sneak under it and weight down with a rock or brick. Tender crowns will stay dry and the holes in the pot will allow any excess heat to vent out. Remove the cover when grass has turned green but keep it handy in case of a late freeze. (This method will protect any tender plants in the winter, including those that aren't hardy in your zone.)

You don't have room to store geraniums over the winter

• Remove the plants from their pots, tie strings around the root balls, and hang the plants upside down in a cool place, such as a root cellar or basement. Don't water. In the spring, remove the strings, replant them, cut them back, and water well. Add fertilizer when they start sprouting leaves.

There is no place to winterize plants

• You can create your own root cellar in a basement to winterize fragile plants while they're dormant. Ideally, the room would have at least one (preferably two) outside walls, a window, and insulation on all four sides. Open a hole in the side of the house as you would for a dryer vent, bring in a hose and pass it down through the ceiling of the insulated room. Attach a small fan to the hose and attach the fan to a thermostat set to the appropriate temperature, which is 35–40º F, so that when the room gets too warm, the fan turns on and brings in some cold air as needed.

Trees don't survive the winter

• Be sure to water young trees and evergreens thoroughly before the ground freezes, especially if the fall has been dry. Keep the hose out as late in the fall as possible and water deeply. If you can't water everything, concentrate on young plantings and evergreens. Light rain won't sustain them, but mature trees will survive dry spells.

• If you must replace dead evergreens in northern climates, use Diablo Ninebark, whose burgundy foliage makes quite a statement. With very prominent clusters of white flowers in June, the shrubs can grow to over 10' tall and 8' across, but a new compact version is just about 6' overall. Hardy to zone 3.

• Instead of tossing a dead evergreen or Christmas tree, put it in the garden. In the spring, plant sweet peas, morning glories, and nasturtiums around the base. The branches gradually lose their needles, but the tree will retain its shape. It's perfect for climbers to grow on.

Cold weather threatens plants in a cold frame

• You can control the temperature in the cold frame. Place it near a window, then fill an old crockpot with water and place it in the cold frame. Run a three-prong outdoor extension cord from inside the house to the crockpot, and on cold nights turn the pot on High. You'll keep the plants warm.

Chapter 9
Wildlife and Birds

Don't You Hate It When...

Bunnies and squirrels are stealing your crops

• Spray the plants with hot pepper wax, made of wax and cayenne pepper, available at most garden stores. Once they take a bite, they'll move on. The wax is safe to use on edibles.

• Poke three or four wooden stakes or twigs into the ground around the plant, then cover each plant with a plastic mesh onion bag.

Cats are digging in the plants

• Stick lengths of bamboo stakes around the plant base.

• Cats don't like sticky stuff, so smear some petroleum jelly on the sticks, too.

• If cats are chewing on (or digging in) the plants, spray them (or the soil of large house-plants) with hot pepper wax spray. It won't hurt the cat but it will make the plants taste bad. Once the cat licks it off its paws after digging, he won't dig in the same spot again.

• Another way to deter cats is to lay chicken wire flat on the ground around the garden. Pin it in place so that it doesn't roll up, but don't secure it tightly to the ground. It needs to move a little.

Cats will not walk on this loose wire for fear of getting a foot tangled in it. Other four-legged creatures—though not dogs—will also be deterred.

Chipmunks are invading

• Shove a wad of cat or dog hair into the chipmunk holes, and they'll take off. (You'll have to figure out where to get such a wad of hair.)

Dogs are a nuisance

• Remove the cardboard from wire hangers, straighten out the hooks and bend the sides to make a double hoop. Push these into the soil throughout the bed. Use enough hangers so the dog can't find enough space to lie down.

• Train a dog to stop digging by spreading some cayenne pepper or citronella in his favorite spots.

Deer are nibbling at your garden

• Try interplanting: Plant aromatic herbs along with flowering ground covers along the edges of garden beds. Deer don't like herbs.

• Or plant flowers deer don't like, such as iris, daffodils, vinca, dianthus, dusty miller, foxglove, purple coneflower, coreopsis, zinnias. They'll leave these alone unless there is no other food available.

9 Wildlife and Birds

• A combination of light and sound will also keep deer away. You need a 7' pole; an outdoor floodlight, a motion-activated, dual-socket floodlight fixture, and a screw-in electric receptacle; and a waterproof, portable radio. Mount the socket fixture onto the pole, and screw the floodlight into one socket and the electric receptacle on the other. Attach the radio to the pole, plug it into the receptacle, and tune it to whatever station that broadcasts the most irritating talk radio. The motion detector should be at the shortest time setting, and the garden should be in a 60' sensitivity range. Deer who venture too close will be startled away by the light and the noise. (Or open a drive-in movie in your yard.)

• Try this low-budget, gardener-approved formula. In a saucepan, combine 4 tablespoons ground cayenne pepper with 1 cup white vinegar and bring mixture to a boil. Boil for a minute, then strain it through cheesecloth or a coffee filter. Puree 1 cup of peeled garlic with 2 cups of water in a blender, and strain the mixture through another coffee filter. Combine both strained mixtures with 1 cup clear ammonia and 1 cup Murphy Oil Soap in a 3-gallon garden sprayer. Fill with the maximum amount of water, then drop in a bar of Ivory Soap. (Optional, but it adds stickiness. Let it dissolve slowly.) Spray this mixture around the areas you want to protect. Reapply weekly and after every rainstorm.

• Or adopt a dog. Of course if you get a dachshund, any terriers, a Siberian husky, or other breed that likes to dig, they'll disturb your garden also.

Deer feast on your tulips

• Since deer love tulips and hate daffodils, plant them together to fool the deer. Plant the late-blooming daffodils on the outside edges and the tulips in the middle. Not foolproof, but worth a try.

Deer are attacking your trees

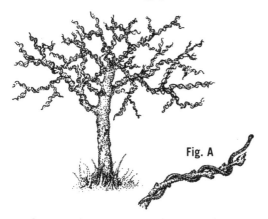

Fig. A

• Deer won't eat through wire. Wrap 20-gauge steel wire loosely around branches, starting about 6" from the trunk. Continue until you're about 1' beyond the edge of the branch.

Once the wire weathers and turns gray, it will hardly be noticeable.

• Or wrap your Christmas tree lights around the branches.

Deer fencing is unattractive

• Spray it with green camouflage paint, available at hardware and sporting-goods stores. It won't be invisible but it will blend better with the surroundings.

• Or use virtually invisible fences. Check out deerbusters.com.

Mice or other rodents are living in a garage or garden shed

• Pour a small amount of pure peppermint oil into several containers and leave them in the infested area. That will drive mice away. Then seal up any holes around the building that allow mice to return, and refresh the peppermint oil as needed.

Moles are plaguing you

• Disturbing the spots where moles are building nests in the spring drives away prospective mole parents. Look for mounds of soil that look bigger than the normal mole runs. Dig up those areas and sink empty 1-liter soft drink bottles in the area, leaving the neck about 3–5" above the soil surface. Air passing over the open bottle will cause vibrations that drive away the moles.

• If moles have burrowed in, on a sunny morning, carefully open up the mole run where the soil has been freshly excavated, pour in molasses, and cover the run with a board or other cover that lets a little light into the run. As they attempt to block the light, the moles will encounter the molasses, which will send them packing. Stop them from returning by placing a molasses trap at the end of each run.

• Or mix together 1 quart water, 2 tablespoons of Tabasco sauce, 1 teaspoon chili powder, and 1 tablespoon liquid dish soap. Pour into a mole hole.

• Moles will avoid caster beans or castor-oil plant. You can grow this exotic-looking plant from seed. Sow in a sunny spot in the spring, when the soil is warm. Many mole-repelling products on the market contain caster bean oil.

• Or plant mole plant, also known as caper spurge, an annual that reseeds itself. The smell of its milky sap drives moles away.

• Some people suggest dropping a wad of Big League Chew® (a shredded gum packed in a foil pouch) into a mole hole and covering up the hole. They claim the mole will eat the gum, get stopped up, and die.

• Turn on a small, battery-operated radio, place it in a sealed watertight plastic bag, then bury it in one of the mole tunnels. The noise drives the critters away.

Rabbits chew your small plants to bits

• Poke three or four wooden stakes or twigs into the ground around the plant, then cover each plant with a plastic mesh onion bag.

Raccoons are invading

• Raccoons hate loud noises, such as talk radio, bright lights, and any unexpected movement.

• Or hang strips of Mylar®, old videotape, old CDs, or pie tins around the garden.

• Activated floodlights and sprinklers work for a while, too.

• Since raccoons become accustomed to any of these deterrents, vary what you use and move them around from time to time.

Rodents are chewing on the bark of trees

• Rub the trunks with bitter-apple gel. A plant product sold at pet stores, it keeps puppies from chewing furniture.

Squirrels are digging up window boxes

• Lay bird netting over the soil, tuck the ends of the netting in on the sides, and cut holes through the netting to plant flowers.

• Also, place a handful of bird netting in the center of hanging flower baskets to prevent birds from nesting.

Squirrels dig up bulbs

• Those smart little critters actually watch me planting the fall bulbs, then come down from the trees to steal them as soon as I leave. I trick them by planting the tulip bulbs 10" deep. Most squirrels will not dig down that far.

• Or cover newly planted bulbs with a board or chicken wire. In about a week, the squirrels will have forgotten about the bulbs, so you can remove the covering.

• Pour a handful of sharp crushed gravel over each bulb when you plant it.

• Or plant at dusk. Squirrels bed down early so they won't see you planting. This is not a joke. You'll have no problems with squirrels stealing your bulbs if they don't see you planting them.

• Wrap steel wool around treasured bulbs before planting. The shoots and roots can grow through the wire.

• Pour a handful of sharp crushed gravel over each bulb when you plant it.

• Or wrap each bulb in chicken wire. If you don't have time, just wrap the bulbs you value the most.

Birds prey on newly seeded gardens or ripened fruits

• Aluminum foil, tin pie pans, and old CDs make great bird scares. Tie the foil or pie pan to a string, or string a group of CDs together to form a chain, and hang the items from a tree, a shepherd's hook, or a bamboo pole. Move them around the garden frequently to make them most effective.

• Or use Christmas tree tinsel, tied to stakes that are pushed far enough into the ground so the tinsel is just above ground level.

• Or fasten tinsel to berry bushes or cherry trees about every 3'.

• Or hang red plastic Christmas tree ornaments on your plants before the fruit begins to ripen. When the birds get no results from pecking, they will fly off and leave the plants alone.

Other gardens attract hummingbirds but yours doesn't

• Hummingbirds love red flowers that have a lot of nectar and tubular construction. One of their favorites is cardinal vine, an annual morning glory with dime-sized red trumpets. As many as 20 birds at a time or more may flock to an 8' stretch of cardinal vine-wrapped fencing.

• To supplement the feeding from the flowers, put up a hummingbird feeder and fill with this recipe. In a saucepan, boil 1 part sugar to 4 parts water. Cool, then pour into a hummingbird feeder. (Though red feeders attract hummingbirds, don't use red dye to attract them to the water. It's proven ineffective, and the dye is fatal to the birds.)

Black fungus builds up in the hummingbird feeder

• Wash feeders once every week (or whenever you refill them) with a 1:9 solution of bleach and water.

Mike's Pick:
My Favorite Hummingbird Feeder

• **Make a feeder that never has to be cleaned.**
Attach the stopper from a hamster watering
bottle to a plastic soda bottle that has been
filled with hummingbird sugar water. Once it's
empty, put the empty bottle in the recycle bin
and fill a new clean bottle. (That tip is worth
the price of the book.)

The birdbath keeps going dry

• Put the birdbath near your drip-irrigation
system, run a small hose and dripper up over
the lip of the bath, and secure the hose with
a rock.

Spilled birdseed sprouts under the feeder

• Zap it in the microwave (two minutes per
pound, on high) and it won't sprout.

• Or spread the seeds evenly on a cookie sheet
and bake them at 250° F for 30 minutes.

• Or plant tall ornamental grasses around your
bird feeder. You'll hide the eyesore of the
spilled seeds, and the squirrels will be hesi-
tant to jump up on the feeder.

Don't You Love It When...

you realize the gardening's never done
(and you're glad about it)!

Index

Annuals, planting of 3
Ants. 155-57
Aphids 157
Apple maggots 157-58
Arborvitae, winter protection for 61
Arm protection, gaiters for 105
Ash plant bug. 158
Azaleas 54
Baby monitor 103
Baby's breath. 83
Bark, attacked by rodents 177
"Bark fines" 138
Bee sting, relieving 158-59
Begonias. 14
Bermuda onions, alternative to 41
Big League Chew® 176
Birch leaf miner. 159
Bird scares. 178-79
Birdbaths 180
Birds nesting in window boxes. 177
Birdseed, preventing sprouting of 180
Black spot 146
Blackflies 157
Bloom, too early 2
Bloom, extending 11
Blue spruce. 60
Bonide® All-Season Spray Oil 162
Bonide® Fung-onil 148
Bonide® Mite X 162
Bonide® Stump Out 64
Bonidev Tomato and Blossom Set 51
Borage 153
Border, edging 121
Box elder bugs 159
Budding too early 164
Bulb planter, do-it-yourself 10
Bulbs gardens, how to plant. 8
Bulbs
   depth to plant 7
   early spring 12
   getting bed ready for 9
   identifying when stored 17
   planting small ones quickly 13
   remembering location of 9, 10
   squirrels digging up 177-78
   storing in winter. 15, 16
   three-layer plan for maximum show . . 12
   which end up. 11

Cane borers 160
Cannas, starting indoors 17
Caper spurge 175
Cats 170
Cayenne pepper 155
Chipmunks 170
Clematis 26, 55
Climbing roses 21
Cocoa bean mulch 128-9
Coconut fiber dust 129
Coffee grounds 54
Cold frame, controlling temperature in . 168
Compost bin 120
Composter, do-it-yourself 119
Composting material 118, 119
Composting pile
   doesn't heat up 118
   smelly 119, 120-121
Container plants, suggestions for 77
Containers 76-82
   drying out quickly 80
   inexpensive 76
Cord, rope and twine, storing of 96
Corn gluten 137, 140, 142
Cornfrey 44
Correct time for planting 2
Creeping Charlie 141
Crops, sparse 41
Cut flowers 82-91
Cytospora canker 150
Daffodils 8, 10, 14, 85, 173
Dahlias 14, 15, 18
Damping off fungus 146
Dandelions 137
Daylily roots, separating for planting . . . 3
Dead space
   in daffodil field 8, 14
   in garden 6, 22
   prevention of 14
Deciduous trees, large, moving of . . 62, 63
Deer fencing 174
Deer. 171-174
Dental floss for tying plants 25
Determinate and indeterminate
   tomatoes 29-30
Diatomaceous earth 153
Dirt, tracked indoors 105
Dogs. 171

Drainage 80, 109
 testing soil for 133
Drammatic® Liquid Fish Plant Food .. 124
Dried flowers, caring for 87
DriWater® 92
Dry well 134
Dying foliage, when to pull 14
Epsom salts 124
Evergreens
 choosing of 59
 large, moving of 62, 63
 planting of 60
 recycling 167-68
Felco® 115
Fencing, inexpensive 97
Fertilizer
 application of 123, 125
 "burning" plants 124
 liquid vs. granular 122
 moving heavy bag of 127
 numbers on bag 123
Fieldstone walls, enlivening 6
Floral foam.................... 89-90
Flower-arranging devices 88
Flowers and leaves, drying and
preserving 85-87
Flowers, cut
 extending life of 84
 feeding and watering of 83
 keeping color in 85
 not enough in vase 88
 odor in 83
 stems too short 87
Flowers, cutting in garden 82
Foxglove 85
Frog, substitute for 88
Frost 164, 165
Fusarium 151
Garden carts 116
Garden gloves
 fitting 106
 organizing 106
Garlic..................... 152-53
 growing 42
Geraniums 166
Gilmour® 135
Ginko 57
Gladious 18

Gnats 160
Grapevine 26
Grass
 diseased and drying 52
 growing transplants for 50
 not green enough 53
 not growing fast enough 48
 patches in 49, 50
 repairing urine and salt damage 51
 surviving during drought 53
Ground cover
 bare space in 22
 debris stuck in 22
Garden jeans, repairing knees of 105
Grape hyacinth 9
Hand care 104
Hand tools 112, 113-114
Hanging plant, dripping of 91
Hanging tomato container 28
Hardwood ash 155
Heat-loving plants 2
Heat-resistant plants 165
Herbicide, avoiding collateral
damage with 140-141
Herbicides and fungicides 135-7
Hibiscus 76
Hornets 158-59, 163
Hose guide, do-it-yourself 100-102
Hose
 looks untidy 99
 storing for winter 100
 prolonging life of 98
Hot spots 6
Houseplants,
 dropping leaves 93
 growing unevenly 94
 insects coming in on 92
 insufficient light for 93
 low-light tolerant 93-4
 pruning too-tall................ 94
 watering while away 92
 watering 93
Hummingbirds 179
Hummingbird feeders, cleaning of ... 179
Impatiens 165
Iris rhizome, marking 17
Japanese beetles............... 160
Japanese spurge.................. 23

183

Index

Kids' garden 76
Lasagna Gardening 134
Lavender look-alikes 4
Lavender 3
Lawn, patching 49, 50
Lawn, testing for traffic readiness 48
Lawns 48-54
Leaf bag, keeping open 131
Leaf catchers, do-it-yourself 132
Leaf gathering speeding up 131-2
caught in ground cover 133
caught in shrub 133
Leaves, raised bumps on 66
Leaves, yellowing 93, 124, 147-8
Let It Rot 118
Lettuce, ruined in hot weather 28
Lilac, overgrown 55
Lilies 18
Mandella vines 6
Mealy bugs 162
Melons, rotting 44
Mice 174
Mike's Picks
Best Commercial Insect Spray 154
Best Commercial Slug Remedy 161
Best Commercial Spray Pump 135
Best Carrot 46
Best Crabapple Tree 65
Best Ground Cover 23
Best Liquid Fertilizer 124
Best Mulch Mixture 128
Best Organic Lawn Weed Control
and Feritilizer 52
Best Pre-Emergent Herbicide for a
Vegetable Garden 140
Best Soil for Container Plants 79
Best Watering Can 116
Best Way to Protect Evergreens 56
Best Weeder 137
Easiest Canna to Maintain I7
Favorite Hummingbird Feeder 180
Favorite Lily for Shade 19
Hardiest Shade Tree 57
Hardiest Shrub Roses 21
Hardiest Tomato Plant 36
Highest-Quality Pruner 15
Longest-Lasting Hose Reel 101
Best 100% Natural Fertilizer 123

Mildew 148-49
Mint insecticide tea 154
Moles 174-76
Morning glories 23
Moss 106-7 . . . .
Mulch,
appropriate application 128
for winter covering 130
selection and purpose of 127
Mulching, with cheesecloth 49
Mushrooms 51
Myke® 78
Needle blight 149
Neem oil 154
Nematodes 152
No Damp Off® 147
Oak Leaf Mold 78
Oleander 54
Onion juice 155
Onions 42
Osmocote® 116
Ornamental grasses, cleanup of 122
Pachysandra 23
Patio plants 76
Pavers 97
Peas 43
Peat moss 129
Pelletized gypsum 51
Peonies 4
Peony hoop, do-it-yourself 5
Pepper plants, in cool weather 31
Pest control, organic 151-56
Pesticides, mixing proper amount 13
Phlox seedlings 5
Pine trees, turning orange 149
Plant markers, do-it-yourself 102-103
Plant stakes,
do-it-yourself 111-112
not tall enough 112
Plant, tipping of top-heavy 91
Plants, spreading out of control 144
Poisonous mixtures, safe handling of . . 136
Pollen stains 90
Houseplants 91-94
Post Ups® 34
Potatoes 44
Pots, disinfecting 150
Potted perennials, storing unplanted 3

Potted plants, too heavy 77
Potting bench, substitute for 71
Potting soil, replacing 78
Premiere Horticulture® 79
Pruning saw, clogged with tree sap . . . 114
Pruning, technique for 65, 66
Pump spray, unclogging 109
Rabbits 170, 176
Raccoons 176
Radishes 44
Rakes, clog-free 131
Rapid Hose Reel® 101
Renaissance® 52
Rhizophaera needlecast 150
Rhubarb 137, 153
Rock,
   hard to dislodge 126
   too heavy 127
Root cuttings
   filing to grow 68
   sorting of 69
Root rot 149-50
Root-bound plants 81, 94
Rose bush, planting of 21
Roses 19-22
   not thriving 20
   propogating of I9
Russian sage 165
Salt damage 51
Salt spray 65
Scale 162
Screening and privacy 24
Seedlings 73-74
   broadcasting technique for 49
   timetable for 49
   distinguishing from weeds 74
   marking of 102
   small tools for 112
   starting in sun 74
   strengthening of 74
   watering of 73
Seeds
   amount to use for grass 50
   containers for starting 70, 72
   eaten by birds 49
   marking, when started outdoors 73
   starting in corduroy 72
   storing leftover 69-70

tiny, planting of 71
washing away 49
Shady areas, vegetables in 41
Shoes, covered with mud 105
Show on a budget 8
Shrub or small tree, too heavy to move 127
Shrub roses 20
Shrubs 54-57
   browning in winter 56
   moving of 63
   non-blooming 55
Sink, outdoor makeshift 104
Sluggo® 161
Slugs 161
Smith and Hawken® 137
Soaker hoses 98, 126
Sod, removal of 52
Soft crowns, protecting from cold 165
Soil Moist® 81
Soil
   clay 133
   loamy, do-it-yourself 134
   readiness for planting vegetables 39
   when ready for garden work 48
Spider mites 162
Spirea 26
Spray bottles, marking` 135
Sprays, mixing of 136
Sprinklers 110
Spruce tress, fungal disease in 150
Squash, rotting 44
Squirrels 170, 177-78
Stinging nettle 142
Stings, relieving 158-59
Stone mulch, cleaning of 129
Strawberries, growing in container 45
Sun scale, protection from 58
Sweet potato vines 25
Terra-cotta pots 106-109
Thorns 20
"Three sisters" 38
Toads for pest control 151
Tomatoes 28-38, 125
   choosing 29
   cut while growing 35
   in cool weather 31
   jump starting 33
   labeling 29

Index

ripening 36
rotting on the vine 35-36
starting up 30, 32, 33
trellis for 34
watering roots of 40
Tools 112-114
caddy 113
cleaning of 114
storage of 113
Topsy Turvy® 28
Trees 57-66
Tree seedlings, removal of 143
Tree stump, removal of 64, 65
"Trellis buddies" 26
Trimming shrubs, cleanup of 122
Tulips 14, 16, 173, 177
Twine 97
Tying plants 25
Urine damage 51
Vegetables
cleaning quickly 45
expanding space 38
for shady areas 41
harvesting guidelines 46
open patches in garden 39
pesticides for 155
sparse crops 41
thirsty crops 41
Vermiculite 69
Verticillum 151
Vines box, support for 25
sweet potato, winterizing 25
won't climb a post 26

Vine-X® Vine & Brush Control 142
Walkways, growing moss on 106-107
Wall-O-Water® 32
Wasps 158-59, 162-63, 158-59
Watering cans 116
Watering houseplants while away 92
Watering
ensuring continuous 40
ideal amount 125-6
remembering to turn off hose 126
WD-40® 105, 114
Weed containers 142
Weeds and soil correction remedies 143-44
control 139
in new soil 138
marking during mowing 54
organic 137, 141
on vines and trees 142
Weeding, timetable for 53
Wheelbarrow handles cut into
your hands 115
Wheelbarrow, rust 115
Whiteflies 157, 162
Willow water 68
Wilt disease 151
Wilt-Pruf® 56, 57
Window boxes 81
Winterizing
begonias and dahlias 15
tender plants 165-66, 168
trees 167-168
Wire baskets, relining 80